Summer Rainbows
Sarah E. Warne

Summer Rainbows
by Sarah E. Warne

First published 2024

© Sarah E. Warne

The right of Sarah E. Warne to be identified as the author of this work has been asserted by her in accordance with the Copyright, Designs and Patents Act 1988.

All rights reserved. No part of this publication may be reproduced, stored in or introduced into a retrieval system, or transmitted, in any form, or by any means (electronic, mechanical, photocopying, recording or otherwise) without the prior written permission of the publisher. Any person who does any unauthorised act in relation to this publication may be liable to criminal prosecution and civil claims for damages.

Cover painting by Jussie E. Lilliot

This book is sold subject to the condition that it shall not, by way of trade or otherwise, be lent, re-sold, hired out, or otherwise circulated without the publisher's prior consent in any form of binding or cover other than that in which it is published and without a similar condition including this condition being imposed on the subsequent purchaser.

ISBN: 9798878357531
Independently Published

The book is dedicated to my Gran
Hilda May Moss (née Lilliot),
April 30th 1892- 27th March 1979.

Also, to all people who have fled their homes and belongings due to war, religion and natural disasters.

Note: The family name *Lilliott* has interchangeably been spelled *Lilliot* over the centuries.

Part 1
Introduction
An extract from *That Summer*
by Jussie E. Lilliot

One day, while brushing Mother's lovely hair out, I asked her about her life. This is what she told me.

Her grandparents, The Lilliotts, were descended from Huguenots who came over from France in the 16th century, and landing at Dover, they set about farming in the Sandwich area of Kent. Mother was born at Sheerwater Farm, Ash East Kent, in a red-roofed, early 18th-century farmhouse deep in the heart of the Kentish Countryside.

Sheerwater Farm

One of eight surviving children, she had a Christian upbringing such as 'grace before meals' and 'regular worship.' Her father, Thomas Southee Lilliott, was a god-fearing man who tramped the surrounding hamlets of Ash with a huge Bible under his arm. Mother referred to him as a good, kind man who gave away more than he made on the farm.

Sarah Ann Castle, her Mother, made everything from butter to bedspreads. She was clever with her needle and thread and made all of the clothes, suits for the boys, and tucked dresses for the girls with pinafores over. At harvest time, she would help to take jugs of cold tea to the harvesters working in her father's fields. She remembered her father cutting the corn with a scythe.

Mother was brought up amid plenty in her early years, but all that changed when Thomas Southee fell ill. First, he lost his sight, then the farm. From the farm, they went to live in Yew Tree Cottage in Upstreet, where she went into service after leaving school. On regaining his sight, Thomas Southee went to work for his brother Joseph, who had a farm at nearby Grove.

After years of hard work, Mother's parents died poor and lay in unmarked graves in Ash Churchyard, Kent.

Chapter One

It was 1985: my mum Joyce Warne, nee Moss, was excited; the parcel she was expecting had arrived. She ripped at the tightly wrapped brown paper with her beautifully manicured fingernails. The delivery in question contained a book not so dissimilar to the Yellow Pages. Instead of names and addresses, this book had people's names, birth dates, deaths, who they married, and the number of children they had.
Doris, Dad's sister-in-law, would visit Somerset House in London and research family history. His family tree was so intriguing that Mum also wanted her Mother's family tree traced, as when she was alive, she had told my mum her family was of Huguenot descendants.

Huguenots were French Protestants in the 16th and 17th centuries who had followed the teachings of theologian John Calvin. In 1572, over 10,000 Huguenot Protestants were murdered within two months; it had started in Paris and was named The Massacre of St Bartholomew's Day, causing many Huguenots to flee to England. Then, in the 1680s, when King Louis XIV changed the law of protection for Protestants, Huguenots were attacked again and fled from France, where more journeyed to England. Many arrived in the ports of Kent and Canterbury, where Calvinism was well-established. They were granted asylum and settled quite happily without the fear of persecution.

Huguenots were the first boat people to arrive in the British Isles. It was when "Refugee" was used for the first time in the English, Language.

Our family's Huguenot surname was Lilliott, my Gran Moss's maiden name. Our ancestors, the Lilliotts, were farmers and had first set up farming in Sandwich, Kent. Over time, they moved their farms inland eastwards towards Ash, supplying Covent Garden with flowers, fruit, and vegetables. Lavender, cauliflower, and strawberries were the largest of their distributions.

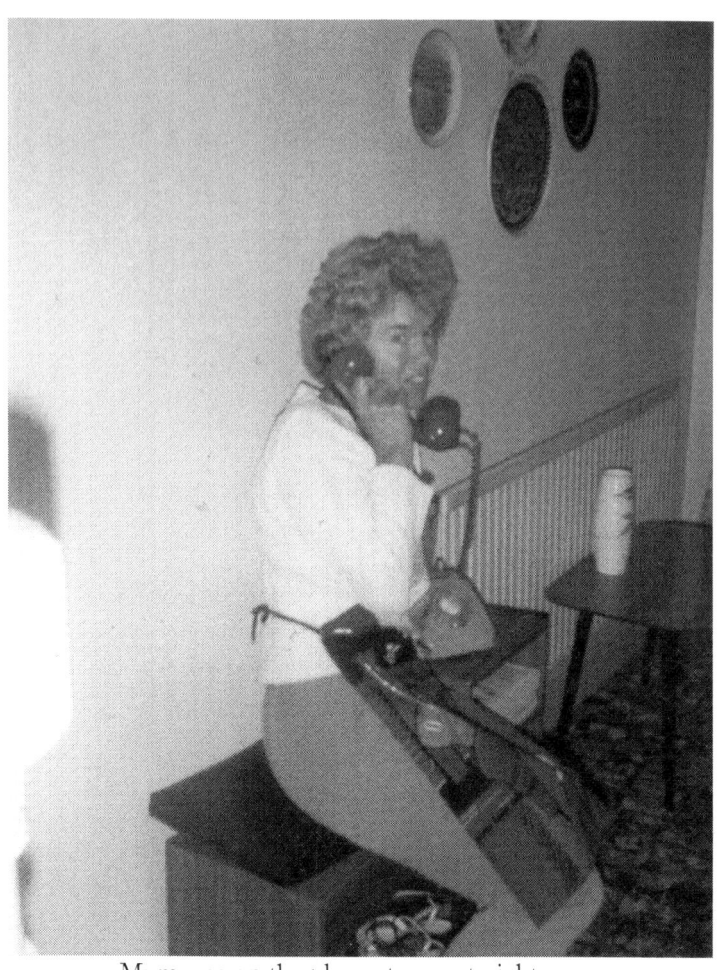

Mum was on the phone to me straight away.

"Sarah Darling", she said. I could almost hear the stammer in the conversation, although it had been under control since she was a teenager. It had come about from sickness and trauma as a young girl, but when Mum spoke with excitement, I could often detect the pause for a breath and to slow down, rethink, and then slowly carry on with her conversation.

"When you visit, I have lots to share with you," She paused again. "Your Aunty Doris has researched my Mother's family tree, which I've just received in the post."

I parked outside my parents' home in Kingsbridge Road, Newbury. It was a detached three-bedroom house; they had lived there since marriage in 1957. Dad had worked for Paines brothers, a men's retail outfitter owned by two brothers of that surname. They had let my parents live in one of their properties. When the brothers passed away, they had gifted the house to Dad in their will. As I emerged from my bright red 2000cc mini car, Mum must have looked out for me as the front door flew open. She smiled her million-dollar smile. She was fifty-four years old, five foot three, very dainty and pretty, with her pure heartedness and fun ways. No wonder Dad had fallen in love with her at first sight.

I was an only child, and my parents had wanted more children. When I was born, Mum was thirty-two years old, and Dad was thirty-six, both from hardship backgrounds. I had had a privileged childhood, filled with love and doting almost too much, but Mum had said she never wanted me to go without like she had.

Dad was in the kitchen making a pot of tea.
"Alright, Saz?" He asked as he turned around.
Dad had a lovely, kind smile and blue-grey eyes.
"Huguenot, eh? I wondered how you had picked up French so well", he had joked.
I was five years old when I started learning French, and I could read, speak, and write fluently. It amazed my parents.
"Look at this family tree, Sarah Darling," said Mum, butting into the conversation. I picked up the many pages of names and dates that date back to the seventeenth century.
"Look at all the names and so many Sarahs."
What a coincidence. There was so much to read and to take in. Mum picked up the document and started to read down the lengthy lists of names written in a scrawled handwriting of black ink.
"Look here!" Mum said, looking directly at her mother's name, Hilda May Lilliott, who was born in 1891.
"Your Aunty Doris has researched the correct Lilliott family."
Mum pointed to my gran's name and the names of her parents and siblings.

"Mother had said that one of her sisters, Rose, had married a Frank Leaver." Said Mum, "They emigrated to Western Australia and had set up farming over there." She paused, then added "They sent us food parcels during WW2. I also remember being told they had a son." Mum was thrilled. I nodded and smiled to show interest and agreed with her, but I wasn't that interested at the time and had never heard of Huguenot.

Mum missed me terribly when I moved out, making a void, adding to the one she had already when her Mother had passed away six years prior. It was a shock for the family. My grandmother, or Mother, as my mum and her siblings called her, had kept everyone and things together. She was the tower of strength and the centre of the family.
Most weekends, my gran, aunts, uncles, cousins, and I would go for a picnic and visit the zoo or the seaside. Some Saturday evenings, we would play card games such as Nap, New Market, and Sevens until the early hours. My cousins and I had such a fun-filled childhood when Gran was alive.

Mum made copies of our ancestry to give to her sisters and my cousins. Joan was her eldest sister with three grown-up married daughters, Cynthia and twins Sally and Jane. Then came Ken. News like this would interest him less. He liked to live in the now and wasn't interested in the past. Then there was Betty with two grown-up children, David, who had emigrated to Canada, and Julie, who lived locally. My mum Joyce - whose nickname was Jussie - was next in line, and then the youngest was Mavis, who also had adult children, Christopher and Alison.

Over the next few days, Mum was on a roll getting our ancestry photocopied and phoning her sisters. Eventually, she put together an individual folder containing the Lilliott family tree for everyone. We arranged to meet at Joan's house in Kintbury, a picturesque village in West Berkshire.

When my aunts and some of my cousins arrived, we all gathered around the large wooden kitchen table. A few years prior, we would meet here for our family get-togethers. It could tell a tale or two. Aunty Joan welcomed everyone with mugs of tea and homemade fruit cake served on China plates and passed around. One could feel the loving energy in the room. Mum handed around the photocopies of the thick family tree. Everyone was most interested. After reading the document, it looked like most families from the Lilliotts had carried the same Christian names through the generations. What with so many births, second marriages, and cousins who had married second cousins? We all found it very confusing to follow who was who.

"So, who exactly were the Huguenots?" asked Betty.
Doris had explained that the Protestant Reformation had an impact throughout Europe in the early sixteenth century. The origin of the word Huguenot is unclear, but it had been the name given to these protestants mainly by their enemies, and Huguenot had stuck.
It was all exciting.

Aunty Joan, though, had the biggest surprise. Twice a week, she would go to "Gran's House." we still called it. Uncle Ken had always lived with Gran, never marrying nor moving out of the family home when Gran passed away. Aunty Joan would do her brother's washing and ironing. She also cleaned and cooked for him. In conversation, Joan mentioned to him the Lilliott family tree being of Huguenot descent and explained to Ken who the Huguenots were and were of the Reformed Church of France who were followers of John Calvin. They had become the major Protestant sect in France. Uncle Ken was surprisingly interested and told her that a large, old wooden box in the cupboard under the stairs contained family history and photos their Mother had left. She was welcome to take the box and may find out more about our family history. He hadn't even looked at it, but Mother had mentioned the contents many years ago. He didn't want anything returned as it took up too much space.

Aunty Joan emptied the contents of the box onto the kitchen table. Everyone was amazed and taken aback. The container spilled out photos and letters written to their Mother, Hilda May, from her brother and some of her sisters, addresses included on a few. Gran's keepsakes. At the top of the pile was a fading slip of paper. It was a list written in black ink in fading scrawled handwriting.

> Thomas Southee Lilliott born at Westmarsh
> in 1860
> Married Sarah Ann Castle (Born in 1859)
> Married at Sandwich P. Methodist Church in 1881
> Children from marriage as follows
>
> | | | Born |
> |---|---|---|
> | Rosa Jane Lilliott | | 1882 |
> | Frederick " | | 1886 |
> | William Edward " | | 1887 |
> | Percy John " | at Sheerwater | 1889 |
> | Hilda May " | at Sheerwater | 1891 |
> | Annie Ellen " | at Sheerwater | 1892 |
> | Sydney Joseph " | at Sheerwater | 1893 |
> | Alfred | Born Feb 6th died Feb 9th | 1895 |
> | Frank Lilliott | Born 6th died Feb 9th | 1895 |
> | Ruth Lilliott ? | | 1896 |
> | Girl. | Still Born | 1898 |
> | Edward Horton Lilliott | Lived 1 month | 1899 |
> | Boy | Died at Birth | 190? |

The room went quiet. Never had I felt so much stillness.

"Gosh!" said Mum, who broke the silence first. She let out a sigh.

"How sad. That our grandmother Sarah Ann Castle lost all those children and also twins."

"And to be constantly pregnant," added Mavis.

"Tragic," replied Joan. She added. "I remember when Mother and Dad's first child, Doris, died. She was only one year old. She caught a chill that had gone onto her chest and then died of pneumonia. Eighteen months later, Ronnie, who was eight years old, caught meningitis and also passed away. I lost my older brother and my baby sister when I was six years old."

My gran had often spoken of Ronnie. His parting had left her heart stricken with grief, the blonde-haired little boy with ringlets who was as bright as a button and just as kind with it. He would come home from school and would love to show how well he could read and write. He sang like an angel, often singing "Away in a Manger" to her. Aunty Joan remembered him well. Gran said she had gone white overnight. Something had just died in her that day. With the loss of two children eighteen months apart, she and her husband Henry had both struggled so hard emotionally. They said they had to adapt; they had their Joan, and Ken had just been born. But they would daily visit their children's graves at Kingston Cemetery Portsmouth. The two children share a grave and lie to rest by a sheltered wall. It took quite a few years for Gran to stop laying a place for Ronnie at the dining table. The loss and grief had caused so much suffering that she had said that a light from her had gone out and seemed to have died with him. The shock had also affected her eyesight. She had started to go blind from the trauma.

"I just couldn't imagine it," said Cynthia.

We tried to move on from the subject and decided to carry on delving into the contents.

"I wonder what other history will surface from this box?"

We all looked around at each other, slightly anxious- but excited to discover the secrets of the unknown wonders that our family history was unfolding. Next, there was a sepia and white side portrait of my Gran, at twenty-one years old.

Then, a photograph of two girls dressed in plain-looking clothes, almost Quaker-like. On the back, it read Nan and Ruth?

"I wonder why there is a question mark after Ruth's name?" Asked Julie.

"No idea," Replied Joan. "But I do know Mother had a relation called Nan and a sister called Ruth."

The following photograph showed a couple looking down adoringly at a baby wearing a long white gown. It looked like a christening photograph. On the back, read Nan and Hubby.

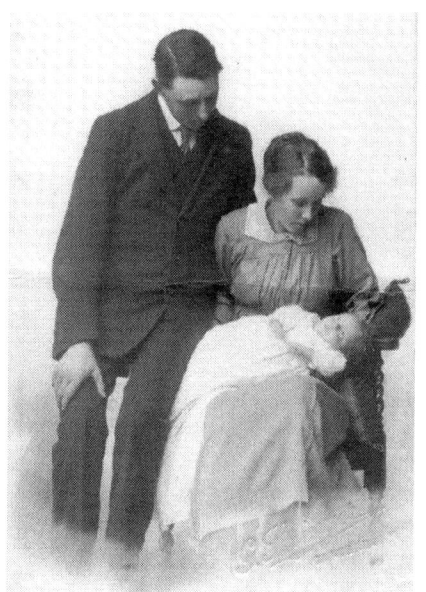

Mum reached forward and picked up a large photo. "Well!" said Mum, quite astonished.

"I remember this photograph very well." The large photograph was a portrait in sepia, showing a distinguished gentleman standing in a straight posture next to an elegant lady sitting in a chair.

Thomas Southee Lilliot and Sarah Ann Castle

"This is a photo of our grandparents. Thomas Southee Lilliot and Sarah Ann Castle. Well, I never have," Mum said. "It's the photograph that Mother had on the mantelpiece next to that annoying clock," chuckled Betty. "The clock which had chimed every quarter of the hour."
"What's this?" asked Julie, picking up a black and white postcard of a jetty.
"I've no idea, Julie," answered Mavis.

On the back was written, *Westmarsh from the Pastures. 1900.*

Another black and white postcard showed people standing with their produce. It read on the front.

Hop-picking at Uphouseden, Westmarsh. On the back the date read 1908.

There was so much to see and so many questions but no answers.

"I do remember this couple," said Joan, picking up a small black and white photo of a couple's head and shoulders. On the back of the photograph was written *Sept 1909. Taken at Tenterden.*

Frank William Leaver and Rose Jane Lilliot.

Here is a photograph of Mother's sister, Rose. She married Frank Leaver, and both emigrated to Australia. They were the couple who sent us food parcels during WW2 when we had food rationing."

"Yes," said Mum, "Those food parcels of tinned meat, jam, honey, bacon, and fat all wrapped up in brown paper and string."

"Those rationing days," said Betty, "How did we manage? Look here!" she said. Picking up a letter, "There are a few letters from them and an address. I also think they had a son."

A postcard showing a black and white photo of a bungalow was next under the pile, and written on the back was an address and date: *The Homestead Farm, Byford, Western Australia, Aug 1949*

A handwritten note on the back read,

The windows left to right
Laundry, bathroom, kitchen, back door, spare room, boys room, window partly hidden by a mulberry tree.
This tree is full of new leaves today (Oct 28th)
The post on the right is a telephone post, it comes into the house from there.
The wires seen are from the electric light.
This is the back way. Someday I will send the front of the house.

"Look!" Exclaimed Julie.
"Here is a copy of the list of passengers, the ship, and the date they emigrated to Australia.
Twin Screw Steamer" BELGIC 10,150 Tons.
Sailing from Liverpool, October 11th, 1912. FREMANTLE.
WESTERN AUSTRALIA.

Twin Screw Steamer " BELGIC," 10,150 Tons.

SAILING FROM LIVERPOOL, OCTOBER 11th, 1912.

Commander : J. H. A. THORNTON.

Surgeon : E. L. BARTLETT. Asst. Surgeon : E. C. JENNINGS.
M.R.C.S. (England); L.M.C.S. (Ireland)
L.R.C.P. (London). L.R.C.P. (Ireland)

Steward-in-Charge : J. B. MALCOLM.

LIST OF PASSENGERS.

To FREMANTLE (Western Australia).

Abercromby, Mrs. Ruth
Abercromby, Miss Ruth
Abercromby, Miss K.
Abercromby, Master R.
Adams, Miss G. M.
Ahearn, Mr. Arthur
Ahearn, Mrs. Kate
  and Infant
Allen, Miss Georgina
Allen, Mrs. Mary
  and Infant
Allen, Miss Louisa
Allen, Miss Annie
Allen, Miss Jeanie
Allen, Master A.

Ambler, Mr. Frank
Ambler, Master D.
Ambler, Mr. Bertram
Ambler, Mr. Harry
Ambler, Miss Ann E.
Anderson, Mr James
Andrews, Mr. William
Andrews, Mr. Herbert
Applin, Mr. Thomas E.
Applin, Mr. Edward
Applin, Mr. Robert
Applin, Master George
Applin, Mrs. Agnes
Applin, Miss Amelia
Applin, Miss Lillian

Kilpatrick, Miss Mary
Kilpatrick, Miss Jane
King, Mrs. Jane
  and Infant
Knox, Mrs. Marie
Knox, Miss Winifred

Law, Mrs. Frances
  and Infant
Law, Miss Alice
Law, Miss Frances
Law, Master Thomas
Law, Master James
Lawler, Mr. Arthur C.
Lawler, Master L.
Lawler, Master Leslie
Lawler, Mrs. Margaret
  and Infant
Lawler, Miss Vera
Lawler, Master Thomas
Leaver, Mr. Frank W.
Leaver, Mrs. Rose J.
  and Infant
Ledger, Miss Mary
Lernan, Miss Agnes
Leslie, Mr. Alex.
Light, Mr. James
Light, Mrs. K.
Light, Miss Annie

Lindsay, Mr. James
Lindsay, Master Alex.
Lindsay, Mrs. Margaret
Lindsay, Miss Rosanna
Lindsay, Master James
Lindsay, Master John
Longson, Mr. Joseph
Longson, Miss Ada L.
Lonsdale, Mrs. Sarah
Lonsdale, Miss Ann L
Lonsdale, Master Wm.
Lorimer, Mrs. Annie
  and Infant
Lorimer, Miss Maggie
Lorimer, Miss Maybeth
Lorimer, Miss Nettie
Lovelock, Mr. James
Lowth, Master Samuel
Lowth, Master Cyril
Lowth, Master Harold
Lowth, Mrs. Ann
Lowth, Miss Emily
Lowth, Master William

Mackay, Mr. Hugh
Mackay, Mrs. Elizabeth
Mackay, Miss Lizzie

"Here are their names, Mr. Frank W LEAVER. Mrs. Rose J LEAVER, and infant." pointed out Julie.

"Good God," said Aunty Joan. "The same year as The Titanic sank."

"Gran had a cousin that went down on The Titanic," said Cynthia.

The White Star Line owned the ship The SS Belgic. It was the third to bear the name Belgic. The vessel took immigrants travelling between the UK and Australia.

Belgic's second voyage to Australia was supposed to sail from Liverpool on March 23rd, 1912, but the journey, due to a national coal strike in Britain, had been postponed. The coal strike affected the schedule of many ships due to their lack of fuel, and some passengers were transferred from other vessels to the maiden voyage of the Titanic, which sailed soon after the strike ended. The Belgic eventually set sail on April 27th, 1912, and arrived at Fremantle, Australia, for the second time on June 11th.

"This must be a school photo of Mother as a little girl," said Aunty Mavis. "Mother had described she would wear clothes like this to school,"

Looking at a classroom of solemn children. The girls wore black pinafores over long white dresses and would wear black lace-up black boots. The boys wore trousers, jackets, and cravats.

The back of the photograph read Top row, first, from the right, Hilda May Lilliott, aged seven years old.

Class photograph-1899.

"The Victorian Days." She said.

"Mother said she and her sisters would wear a handkerchief pinned to their pinafores."

"Yes," said Joan. "Mother also mentioned. They would have strawberry and cream teas. The freshly picked fruits would be put on trestle tables in a barn. For a sixpence, they could eat all they wanted!"

There was another address, this time on the back of a photo reading Frederick.

from Upstreet.

"Gran's brother Fred," said Julie.

Again, Mum wrote down the address.

"He won't be alive, Auntie Joyce; he would be over a hundred years old!"

Mum replied, explaining she would write to the residents of the above addresses to ask if they had any information about the family.

"Upstreet wasn't far from Chislet," said Mum. "It's also where Mother told us it was where she married our dad, Henry Moss."

We all nodded in agreement.

The following photograph showed a black-and-white photo of a large farmhouse with a large barn. My Gran's unmistakable handwriting read *Sheerwater Farm. On the road from Elmstone Church.*

"This is the Farmhouse where Mother said she was born," said Mum." She had said it was in Ash, East Kent. The farmhouse had a red roof, early eighteenth century, and was deep in the heart of the Kentish Countryside."
"What a beautiful looking farmhouse set in such an idyllic surrounding," said Betty." It's almost as if she has left it here for us to find and visit."
"Here, Julie," said Mum, holding up a photograph of a jetty.
The front of the black and white picture showed two men on a chain raft. In the bottom left-hand corner was written. *Grove Ferry*.

On the back was written *Grove Ferry 1903*.

"I wonder if this is The Ferryman? Mother mentioned her father, Thomas Southee, and his brother Joseph Lilliott would transport their produce from here." Then, the room turned quiet when the sisters saw the following two photographs. It showed when they lived in Portsmouth before WW2 broke out.
They were in the garden with their Mother.

"Look at this," said Joan. "I remember this photo. We were wearing our Sunday best."

The photo showed them with their Mother, Mavis, sitting on her lap and Ken holding a black and white kitten. A rose tree stood behind them.

"I remember the rose tree," said Mum. "The perfumery is one I'd never forget."

"You must have been about six years old in that photo, Joyce," said Joan.

"Yes," replied Mum, nodding in agreement.

"Our poor Mother," said Mavis.

Everyone nodded.

The second of the two photographs showed Mavis as a toddler on the grass with Mum, Ken, and Betty standing in the front garden. Behind them was an arch adjoining the terraced houses.

"Oh my," said Mum. "I never thought I would see that archway again...Although I'll never forget it either.

The number of times I raced through that archway to get to the dugout when I heard the wail of those sirens."

We decided to leave after another cup of tea and a further discussion of the find. Aunty Joan said Mum could take what she would like to help with her progress to learn more about their family.

All the sisters (my Aunts) had that peaches and cream skin handed down from their mother, Hilda May. They had also inherited her pure heartedness and laughter, Aunty Joan with her Jackie O looks, Mum with her million-dollar smile, and Betty and Mavis with their film star look. No one could have imagined what tales they could tell of their heartaches and hardships when they had become child evacuees during WW2. You would never hear them moan or complain. They just got on with it.

Chapter 2

It was a Sunday evening. Mum was writing letters at the kitchen table. She had always enjoyed writing since I could remember; her handwriting was impeccable. Friends and family often approached to ask her to write their wedding invitations or Birthday and Christmas cards.

Mum would write letters to Dad's sister, Nancy, when she was alive and to her friend Dorothy from No.1 Kingsbridge Road, who had married an American and moved to Florida. She would also write to a great school friend, Pam, who had emigrated to California and would read part of her replies to me telling of blue skies, the warm Californian sun, the sea, and delicious foods. She would look up at me from reading and often sigh.
"Life reads so well out there."
When one wrote to one's friends or family living abroad, The writing paper was much thinner than usual; it was blue and called airmail.
Since her Mother had passed away, Mum had seemed somewhat lost.
"I was only 24 years old when my dad died. He was only 62 years old, Sarah Darling." She would say to me, "He had chronic asthma." She took a sip of tea and looked at me with her soft brown eyes.
"Then, when Mother passed away, although she was a great age at 86 years old. I was only 46 years old. She was 40 years old when I was born and 45 years old when she had your Aunty Mavis. I never imagined life without her. Sometimes, there seems to be such a void."
She would wipe away a tear when she spoke about her parents.
"My poor Mother, she had such a hard life. But, C'mon, enough about me moping. Let's hope I get replies to these letters I've written. I've sent a letter to Sheerwater Farm, where Mother was born, one to Byford Western, Australia, and another to Upstreet, Kent." She had added, with a smile. "I almost forgot to mention, I've entered a competition. The Newbury Weekly News and Tesco are running a Valentine's competition for the best poem. The winner will receive a bottle of champagne and a bouquet."

She took a breath.
"I never win anything. It's just a bit of fun."

Mum was slightly disappointed she had not received any replies to her letters enquiring about the family history. Although she knew it was like looking for a needle in a haystack, she thought that any response would have been better than none. Mum had even written to and sent inquiries to local parishes and councils in and around East Kent asking for anyone in the area with the Lilliotts ' surname. The letters she had posted all contained stamped addressed envelopes for the recipients to send a reply.

It was Valentine's Day. Dad was retired and would give Mum a lift to work. He would drive to St. Michaels Road, where his mum had once lived. Mum would walk to Ginchey Hair, her reception job on Bartholomew Street.

Dad would go back home and make coffee. Every day, he would do the daily mail crossword and time himself. In the evening, he would telephone me when we would compare our times against each other. It was fun.

This particular Valentine's Day, Dad had just started to do the crossword when there was a knock at the door. A lady stood holding a bouquet of red roses and a bottle of champagne.

"Are you Ted?" She asked. He nodded, amused, as she started to recite the poem Mum had written.

> *I've been wed to my husband*
> *Ted for a whole lifetime, so*
> *please send him some roses and*
> *wine, 'cos he's my Valentine.*

This message is brought to you by Tesco Stores & the Newbury Weekly News.

The messenger left the roses, champagne, and the attached poem on a card with Dad. He was speechless and had no idea what was happening; Mum hadn't told him about the competition as it had not entered her mind to think she would ever win.

That evening, Mum phoned me.

"Oooh, Sarah Darling," she said. "Do you remember a few weeks ago, when I mentioned the Valentine poem competition I had entered with Tesco and the Newbury Weekly News? Well," She laughed. "I won! But…" She carried on. "I never mentioned it to your dad, as I never dreamed in a month of Sundays that I would ever actually win!" she exclaimed.

Mum added about Dad's astonishment when he phoned her at work to ask about the Valentine's delivery and poem. She said she had almost fallen off her work stool. Mum also added that there still hadn't been any response from her letters, so she had now written to local schools surrounding the areas of Sheerwater Farm, Westmarsh, and Upstreet of Ash, Kent. She had also written further to the parish in Sandwich. Surely, somewhere, there was some history of the Lilliotts from Huguenot descendants.

A few weeks later, Aunty Mavis, noticing Mum's unusual quietness, had telephoned to say there was a coach trip going to Portsmouth for the day and asked if she would like to join her. Mum and her siblings were born in Portsmouth, and all had been billeted to Hungerford in West Berkshire as child evacuees during WW2. Their brother Ken was always taking the train to Portsmouth, an avid Pompey Football supporter, and although the sisters supported the football team even to the extent of Aunty Mavis, whose front doorbell played *Play Up Pompey, Pompey Play Up* to a tune made by a carillon of bells. None of the sisters had visited their place of birth. Although mum was curious to return and see the area, it had also terrified her as there were memories of fear and high anxieties that she had buried long ago, including the start of her stammer, although now under control, had taken many years to do so. Dad thought it would do her the world of good.

"Sometimes, Jussie," Dad said, "Facing up to these anxieties may do you the whole world of good."

Mum wasn't so sure. She was only nine years old when she and her family fled from Portsmouth with her four sisters, one brother, Mother, and Father. She had only taken one doll. Mother hadn't even taken more than one dress.

Chapter 3

Aunty Mavis and Mum arrived in Portsmouth nervous and excited about what they may find and what memories would surface. She was nine years old, and Mavis had been seven when they left the war-torn city and had no idea if there was anything left to see from their childhood.

They walked in silence but comfortingly arm in arm towards 23. Shore Avenue, only to find that the road was renamed Moorings Way. Opposite, the sea looked as welcoming as ever. When they had lived there, and if the sea had become rough, Mum and her siblings would watch out the window to see the huge waves come in and wash the road, but when the tide went out, and the sea became calm once more, they picked up seashells and paddled in the pools which the sea had left behind. As they strolled along, fun memories and friends came to mind.

"Mave, do you remember?" Smiled Mum, pointing across the way. "My friend Ella Bayley? She had lived on one of the houseboats moored here." Mavis nodded and smiled.

"Yes, her mum put alcohol in everything, even in the gravy."

"Yes," laughed Mum. "Mother's face when she sampled it. Although it tasted delicious, Mother called it "ninety-eight percent!" And we would call Ella's dad Capt'n."

Aunty Mavis replied, saying she remembered the house boat's name as *Summer Drift*.

"I remember, as Mother would always answer when anyone wondered where you were. "Jussie is on the *Summer Drift*. She would say." Mum smiled, "Do you remember Mrs. Bayley invited Mother for a cup of afternoon tea on Summer Drift?" Mavis smiled, and they both went into terrible childlike giggles.

"Oh yes." Laughed Mum, showing her beautiful smile. "How could one forget?"

Extract from Mum's Diaries:

Mother was about to drink her tea when the sea came in swiftly. The boat lurched slightly, and hot tea ended up in her lap.

"People are most welcome to their boat dwellings. Mother had said with good grace. Give me a steady ground. But, Mrs. Bayley thought it was green-eyed jealousy."

Mum and Mavis looked over and realised that the houseboats weren't there anymore, but their house was, complete with the archway that joined with the neighbouring house.

"Through that arch, I had bolted for dear life. One day when I saw the bombers like tiny crosses in the sky. To this day, Mave," said Mum. "I will never forget the distinctive drone of the enemy warcraft." Aunty Mavis nodded in silence, standing in their silence of thought. I shivered in the warm September sunshine remembering the long hours of living in the damp Anderson Shelter or "dug out" as they had called it; it was a corrugated iron structure with three steps going down, much of it was lined with sandbags and just had dirt for a floor. It was in their garden for protection from the bombings. Every night, when their Mother was ready with jugs of steaming cocoa and snacks. As the sirens wailed, seven of us piled into our shelter.

To help dull the noise of the exploding bombs, Dad played the mouth organ as we sang like birds, oldies such as Knees up Mother Brown and Daisy Daisy, just to mention a few. Singing kept our spirits high. Singing kept our spirits up and made us less afraid. At times, we would say that our off-key warbling was enough to send the Luftwaffe packing. In our way, it was an act of defence against them. Sometimes, a lonely neighbour would join us in our shelter to sit by the dim light by torch until the all-clear sounded. Life was a daily round of visits to the shelter, gas mask drills, disruptive school lessons, sirens all clear, blackouts up at the windows before nightfall, and the ever-gnawing fear of the unknown.

I was aware that each day could be my last, for if our shelter had a direct hit, there would be little or no chance of survival. I knew this to be true, and with this realisation came another dread for which I had started to stammer.

Gone was the peace and tranquillity of life as I knew it. It was the norm to sleep nightly in the dugout. Did I say Sleep? Well, try to sleep on those hard benches as the bombs rained down above our heads. The shelter was small and damp and no good for an asthmatic like our poor dad. At dawn, he would emerge ashen and spend his work at the dockyard.
Instead, the things I'd always taken for granted now seemed but a dream.

"C'mon Joyce," smiled Mavis, breaking Mum from her thoughts.

"Let's stroll and take in the lovely sea air."

The sisters stopped here and there and collected a few seashells and smooth pebbles just as keepsakes, a memory. As they walked, taking in old and new surroundings, they stopped suddenly after noticing The Good Companion, their dad's local. It was still on the corner of Eastern Avenue and had withstood all the bombings. The building was a lot larger nowadays with its three extensions, but the original part of the pub was still standing. Both sisters wiped tears from their eyes, remembering when their family had said their goodbyes to their friends at the pub, leaving behind their home and all their mod cons, not knowing where they would be, billeted to. Although they would be back soon.

"It will only be a few months, and we will return!" Their dad, Henry had said. Alas, he and the family never returned.

Mother had decided to evacuate the whole family just while the bombings were so intense in Portsmouth. She didn't realise the Blitz would rage on for many years.

The decision to evacuate us had come about when her life was about by a strange twist of fate, the loss of her purse in The Woolworths on Commercial Road.

Mother had scrimped and saved throughout the year to buy some bits and bobs in the January sales, but her purse had gone. It had got lost somewhere amongst the jostling crowds.

She reported the mishap to the office and started for home. But her journey was halted, as there was an air raid warning. Taking cover in an air raid shelter when Mother had come out, she heard that in the mayhem of that raid, the same chain store - the very one she would have been in had fate not intervened, had been flattened by the bombs.

Then came the mother of all raids on Pompey. It was as though 'they' were trying to bombard us off the face of the earth. We cowered our heads in our make-do shelter, which shook from the blasts. I thought I was going to die. We were all petrified. But then I thought, surely our lives won't end like this after Mother's astonishing escape or whatever you made of it a few days earlier.

After the onslaught, we crawled out, tired and tearful from the dugout. It was frightening to see the skies ablaze red with fire. The smell of acrid black smoke and shrapnel littered the gardens and roads.

Neighbours eventually emerged from their Anderson Shelters. Everyone was terrified after the all-night-long barrage of explosions. We all checked up on each other to make sure all was okay. As overhead, large searchlights scoured the skies for enemy aircraft. But it really wasn't okay.

The Newspapers the next day said it all in large lettering. The headlines read. "PORTSMOUTH SET ON FIRE".

Mother had decided enough was enough and thought evacuating the whole family to the country would do them good. What with her husband Henry invalided from work with asthma and me with my stammer. We children needed a childhood, but not this. Mother had been born and brought up on a farm, and although it had been hard work, her childhood had been peaceful and tranquil, which she had so desired for her children. Being evacuated to the countryside would be the best solution she could come up with.

My gran said she would get a job to send money back to Portsmouth Council to keep their beautiful three-bedroom house. They would only take a few belongings with them and leave the rest behind for when they returned. They said their goodbyes to their friends, saying it was a temporary measure just until the war had finished. Both parents had been upset leaving behind the graves of their two children at the Kingston Cemetery, which they had visited every day.

The family were then billeted to Church House in Hungerford, now known as Croft Hall. Gran took a job working in the kitchen there and sent her wages back to pay for rent for their house in Portsmouth.

After six months, a cottage in Kintbury, just two miles from where they were staying, had been offered to them. It would be a safe haven, somewhere they could stay until the war had ended or a permanent home had become available. She didn't know what to do for the best as they had wanted to return to Portsmouth, back to their friends and lovely house to their belongings and mod cons. But WW2 was still going on strong with no end in sight and unable to afford two lots of rent on two properties. She decided it would be better to give up their lovely Portsmouth home and move into Inglewood Cottage. They would apply for a house back in Portsmouth when the war finished.

The Gentry owned the cottage, which would be a temporary home for the family until the war's end. It was cold and draughty, but they were safe.

Gran still only had one dress, which she would remove at night, wash, and wear the next day. But the biggest challenge was having no running water, just an indoor well in the pantry. They lived in that temporary accommodation with no running water for ten years! After the Second World War, Gran and Grandad had applied to return to Portsmouth, but the council replied there was not enough housing for their return.

Mum and Mavis decided to stop at The Good Companion, order food, and cheer a toast to their dear parents.

The two reminisced about their childhood before the outbreak of WW2 and their visits here at the pub. It was the highlight of a summer evening when they had visited their dad's local, sipping lemonade and munching on crisps. Here in the pub garden, a treat to end all treats.

They spoke about how calm and happy their home had been here and their Mother, the heart of the family. Their lives were untroubled, and their needs were small. Their dad worked in Portsmouth Dockyard, while Gran would make a hot dinner every day followed by suet pudding, of which treacle was the favourite. For Sunday tea, they would have jelly and custard with fancy cakes bought cheap at closing time on a Saturday from the bakers up the road.

They carried on with their reminiscing, sharing laughter mixed with tears of happy and sad memories. Remembering when their parents were both in ill-health and hospitalised. They stayed with their brother Ken and sister Betty at a children's home, The Cottage Homes. Joan, being older, went out to work and managed to keep their family home going while their parents were recovering in different hospitals.

They strolled along Meon Road to see their school, Meon Infant School, which still looked the same. St. Mary's church was next on their list to visit. It was a place where their parents had felt peace amongst themselves. Reverend Allyson had christened them.

"The look on Mother's face when she opened the front door of Inglewood Cottage and saw that the Reverend Allyson had also evacuated to our tiny village in West Berkshire," said Mum. They decided to enter the wondrous church.

"I don't know who was more surprised, him or Mother."

They sat at the back pew to recollect their thoughts of the day and said thanks of prayer for keeping them safe throughout the war-torn City of Pompey during WW2.

The last place they decided they had to visit was Kingston Cemetery. Their Mother had told them the two children had been born and taken away so suddenly within eighteen months of each other. Ronnie and Doris Moss, Doris had been buried in a glass coffin, which their Father had carried. They both shared the same grave against a sheltered wall.

They never expected to find the grave after so many years of at least seventy, but here stood the headstone.

DOROTHY HILDA
1 YEARS OLD
16th SEPTEMBER 1925

RONALD FREDERICK
8 YEARS OLD
14th APRIL 1927

Sheltered against the churchyard wall with the railway line behind. The grave was overgrown with daisies. Both knelt in silence. Mum took a small pair of nail scissors from her black handbag and cut the long grass and weeds leaving the daisies. Mavis got some water from the old rusty tap from the nearby standpipe. The two bought some flowers for the empty rose.

"I'm so glad we visited here," said Mum. "But I never want to return. The childhood memories I had as a child returned so clearly as if it was yesterday, but now is a past that I want to move away from."

Mavis agreed. It had been a long day but one that had been truly dear in every way. They left Portsmouth with memorable days gone by and treasured seashells.

Chapter 4

Mum had decided to do an evening course called Creative Writing at Newbury College and had bought a second-hand typewriter. She tried to self-teach herself to type and was so slow that she half-wrote and half-typed.

It was a small class of ten adult students, with everyone supporting each other's work.

Mum hadn't spoken much about her day trip to Portsmouth, but Dad and I noticed she was leaving notelets around the house when her childhood memories surfaced. When I was visiting, she would ask me if I could recall any stories that I could remember that she had mentioned to me about her childhood.

As I was growing up, Mum often told me tales from her life as an evacuee. Sometimes, these stories were quite fun. As I reminisced about what she had told me, Mum would write it down and add the stories to her own, triggering other memories.

Mum never mentioned another word about all the letters she had posted to discover more about The Lilliotts. One had almost thought she had given up hope. But Dad had said she checked and thoroughly searched all the mail when it dropped through the letterbox. Although Mum loved receiving letters from her friends abroad, the hope of anything from Australia was always there.

Christmas came and went. Mum enjoyed the college course immensely. and even asked for a Christmas present, a Dictaphone or an electric typewriter. Dad had bought her both.

I'd bought her two reams of paper and an ink ribbon for her typewriter - Alas, the electric typewriter was far too heavy for Mum to keep setting up on the dining room table and to put back when not in use in the cupboard under the stairs. It ran too fast for her to type on. On one occasion, the walnut finish on the dining room table became scratched when she lifted the electric typewriter. She never used it again! Mum made do with handwriting and finger typing on the second-hand old machine. Although she was so much slower with typing, using the Dictaphone made everything so much easier, as when thoughts came to mind, the memories could now be recorded and typed in her own time. Although Mum was very slow, she was more comfortable with this setup. She also had to have a pseudonym in college. The students used their childhood nicknames and their mothers' maiden names. Mum's nickname was Jussie, and her mother's maiden name was Lilliott. Using the first letter of her middle name, Eva, JUSSIE E. LILLIOT became her pen name. Prior to this, she had signed her work as Joyce Lilliott-Warne.

January 15th was Mum's birthday, so I bought her a thesaurus. She still hadn't heard anything from her letters, so she decided to re-write to all again and resent self-addressed envelopes. Instead of writing about The Huguenot descendants, Mum wrote about who she was, her mother being born at Shearwater Farm, and her Mothers' siblings only going on from what Mother had told her long ago.

With Mum on the college course, she would write in her spare time. Each week, the group would be given a word and write an essay expressing what it meant to them. In class, they would discuss their written piece from the week before.

**

Light/Dark

One moment, there was light the next, had defied all description. She had plunged into the depth of an abyss so swiftly as though black curtains had been drawn across the eyes, shutting out the light. There was nothing anyone could do. The specialist told her that the blood vessels behind the eyes had collapsed and it would be most unlikely that she would ever see again. She became a registered blind person. At first, she suffered complete desolation of spirit, then very gradually, she began to rebuild her life. She somehow was given the inner strength to see her through the challenging years ahead. On losing her sight, the other senses sharpened considerably. She sensed when things were right or wrong. The biggest drawback was being confined to the house and waiting for someone to accompany her on outings. It was a harrowing experience to suddenly lose one's independence. To be reliant on others was intolerable but forced to be acceptable. She hated pity but loved kindness and understanding.

She said once that no one would ever know the utter despair of not being able to see a loved one or just being able to read a book.

However, there were some lighter moments. Once a month, "The Blind Club" issued her with a talking book. On this occasion, it happened to be "The Black Hole of Calcutta". She was most indignant and told them she wanted to cheer up and, in the future, to be more selective in their choice. She loved the summer when she would once again sit in her striped canvas chair under the lilac tree to enjoy its fragrance. If it was wet and she hadn't been out, she would stand by the open door and (as she put it) breathe in God's fresh air.

She remarked that she had a lot to be thankful for. There were people far worse off than her. Her resources were admirable. She was indeed a woman of courage.
When winter showed its dreaded face and the days were long and lonely, some days she saw not a single soul and would complain of having to sit by the fireside all by herself. She coped amazingly well in the house with all the menial tasks and said that as time passed, one gets used to the darkness, and on rare days, one can almost forget one is blind. I cannot comprehend the statement. Not to see the dawn in all its beauty, birds, trees, flowers, and a fiery sunset would deprive me of nature's most bounteous gifts. Often, she would state her eyes felt tired and sore; she thought that statement might sound strange to some people, but I assured her that it made complete sense. She could see a glimmer of light as the years passed, but it never increased beyond this point. How do I know all this? This brave woman was my Mother, who lost an adorned eight-year-old son to meningitis. She never got over his death and had grieved inwardly for years. Consequently, something had to give, and she lost her sight. Mother is no longer here; she went from light to dark, and now she has gone from dark to light.

* * *

The Jug

The postcard was face down when I turned it over; the picture depicted a jug that sparked childhood memories. I was very young and living in Portsmouth when war broke out in 1939. Pompey, one of the main targets for enemy minecraft, was under a constant barrage of bombardment. Most nights were spent in an Anderson Shelter, and Mother would prepare this giant earthenware jug full to the brim with piping hot chocolate down into the shelter with a bundle of snacks. To help deaden the noise of the bombing, Father would play the accordion, and we would have a singalong. This helped to keep our spirits up and make us less afraid. I missed out on a birthday cake, too. The siren started wailing just as Mother put the cake in the oven, and we all ran into cover and emerged several hours later to find the precious cake had been burnt to a cinder. My family put up with the bombing for two years and then decided to move away. We were tired of spending so much of our lives in the air raid shelter. It was a very frightening experience for us all.

We moved into the peaceful countryside of Berkshire, and Mother insisted the large jug be packed with the utmost care; it was to remind us all that we came through the bombing without a scratch. Others were not so lucky. My parents lost several close friends, and a nephew went down on the HMS Hood. The receptacle was unpacked and used for floral arrangements only.

Today, it stands neglected on a dusty shelf in the shed; it is chipped and cracked and houses several spiders lurking there. I have no further use for it but cannot dispose of it, for it has too many memories.

* * *

Chasing Butterflies

April mist disappeared in the sun. A sparrow building its nest flew back and forth from the hedge to the garden with strands from the aubretia. He kept this ritual for about thirty minutes, flying off each time with a beakfull. A couple of frogs came up to the surface of the small fish pond and sat motionless. With just their heads above water, they looked like hippos sunning themselves. The glorious weather tempted me from my garden into the back lane. The blackthorn was decked with snowy white blossom clouds, and hedges showed green. I noticed the leaf bud on the horse chestnut opening, and a fat bumble bee was busy on the pollen-laden catkins. The path before me was bright gold with dandelions and celandines peeped like saffron stars.

Then I saw a Red Admiral, fragile wings opening and shutting with the delicate movement. This beautiful creature took me back to my childhood.

With friends, we laughed and skipped barefoot over meadows thick with buttercups, chasing butterflies.

The common cabbage white floated over the fields in great numbers. We followed them with our butterfly nets as they meandered over wildflowers and hedgerows. We counted how many species we saw as they fluttered over the countryside. While growing up in the country, butterflies were abundant and constantly graced parks and gardens with their loveliness.

Clouds streaked the sky like satin ribbons as we approached a local wood. Near the entrance was an oak tree where we lingered to swing on a low branch. On several occasions, we picnicked under its green parasol. Bracken crackled under our feet as we tramped into the wood. The trees were so dense in parts that the sunlight could only trickle through like a golden seam. We would pretend that sometimes it was haunted and wicked goblins dwelt under the various fungi that grew there in the dampness. As long as we didn't disturb the plant, we would be safe from their evil spells and come to no harm. The few deers we saw were imaginary dinosaurs. Better keep out of their way; they could be hungry.

There were so many tangled paths, all leading to a sunlit stream. It was a frequented spot and pure enchantment to us. The shallow water trickled lazily over stones as we splashed, paddled, and sought smooth pebbles. We made paper boats and tiny canoes for the wood-fairies. We made them perched on a boulder to devour our paste sandwiches and to drink lemonade, with long legs dangling over and toes reaching into the cool waters. Time stood still for us at this magic place.

We crossed the stream on stepping stones to the steep bank opposite, which was yellow with primroses, and filled our Easter baskets with these fresh spring flowers. A cuckoo called across the wood somewhere; we would mimic him. This would be repeated several times a day, and after a while, it was difficult to distinguish the bird from the imitator.

Hide and seek was a favourite game; we ran carefree through the dappled woods and hid up trees, behind fallen logs, amongst bushes, or in any opening or gap we could find. Very often, it was difficult to find everyone as they lay scattered into the thicket. Sometimes, a rabbit would give the game away, darting from the undergrowth where it had been disturbed. Occasionally, we *doubled back to our starting place, and the tired seeker returned to find us stretched out on the springy turf, grinning ear to ear. The days were endless and full of laughter.*

There was no television, so our spare time was spent in the fresh air, weather permitting. In Autumn, as trees mellowed, the woods were steeped in colour as red, gold, and copper mingled, and underneath, we were ankle-deep in a sea of leaves.

Hazel nuts hung ripe and tempting. It didn't take long to fill a brown carrier bag with them, but by the time we got home, the contents had dropped to half, and we were left with a stomach ache. The same thing applied to the wild strawberries, blackberries, and crab apples we picked.

At home, we had a stone copper in the corner of the scullery, for which I took home kindling wood. As I write this, I can see it all now: Mother amidst the steam, wasps of damp hair curling over her forehead in coils as she toiled over the giant wash tub. With a huge copper stick, she would plunge, twist, and prod at the washing until it was snow-white while the fire billowed away underneath.

Even in Winter, the woodland still held us under its spell and was hauntingly beautiful. Well wrapped up against the chill and eating the hottest peppermints we could buy, that is, if we had any sweet rations left, we went there at every opportunity. If our sweet quota was depleted, we bought Rennies; these were the next things to mint.

Trees stood bare and stark against a pale blue sky. Our beloved stream was still and silent, its ice sparkling in the weak sunlight like a tinsel on a Christmas tree. Sparrows were pecking at iron-hard earth, crows cawed as they circled the bleak and frosty woods, and everywhere was flowerless. It was too cold to loiter, our breath almost froze on our lips, and our chilblains hurt. We walked briskly through frozen paths, stopping only to listen to a robin pouring out his sweet song from a leafless tree. With noses bright red from the intense cold, we would hurry home to a welcoming log fire and hot buttered toast. Gathering around the warm hearth and with hands cupped tight on steaming cups of cocoa, we spoke of days when sunshine would flood the fields and meadows once more, and we would go chasing butterflies.

The Edge of Nowhere

I stopped dead in my tracks; I was on the edge of nowhere. Nowhere, meaning congested traffic that spilled fumes from exhaust pipes- cars are screeching to a halt. Grime blackened buildings. The smoke-filled atmosphere of long queues at bus stops. Non-Melodious music blared out from shop doorways and litter-strewn alleys. I had to escape the pollution and the masses that hemmed me in. I turned in the opposite direction of the town and headed for the healing countryside. I walked with an urgency that I had not felt before. I walked across a wooden bridge and saw a stream glinting in the sunlight; it looked cool and refreshing. The low murmuring of the water as it made its way downstream was like music to my ears. Marsh marigolds with their rich golden blooms were nestling in damp, leafy cradles of green. At the water's edge, the tall, straight flags burst out of the silver-green covers that tightly bound them.

I followed the path by the stream, and nature was here in full array. Creamy cow parsley adorned the banks as far as the eye could see, looking like a beautiful lace mantle. A dragonfly hovered over the water, its transparent wings making it almost ethereal-like.

The hedgerows were intertwined with sweet-smelling honeysuckle and blushing wild roses. The bright dandelions were thickly spread and looked like sheets of gold before me. The exquisite tiny blue speedwell made a lovely show; I knew it as birds-eye as a child. Somewhere across the stream, the cuckoo called, and the abysmal scene that had greeted me in the town less than an hour ago was forgotten.

I walked on and came to a stile that led me to a meadow carpeted with buttercups. There was a majestic oak tree. I sank down on its grassy skirt and leaned against its mighty trunk, the generous canopy of green protecting me from the hot May sunshine. I sat there for some time, hidden from man's gaze, not a human soul in sight—no one to intrude on my solitude or the tranquillity of that moment.

Bees hummed drowsily in the nearby cowslip cups, and once again, the cuckoo called. Feathery wisps of cloud drifted lazily in an azure sky, and there was just a faint whisper of breeze. The distant slope of the meadow was covered in a sea of yellow gorse and looked as if drenched in sunshine. Indeed, God dealt here and locked pollution out!

Stirring myself, I was blissfully aware of the wonders that. I turned and looked at the beautiful Oak tree I had been sitting under and asked myself why man wanted to destroy these marvellous works of natural art. There was a small wood nearby filled with bluebells. Two people walking their dogs had picked a bunch of each of these lovely flowers, but already the bluebells had started to wilt, with their bell-shaped cups on slender stems, these flowers are not shown to their best advantage in a vase where they will soon droop and die. But left to grow in their natural habitat, these beautiful wildflowers will multiply and grace the countryside.

The bird song was coming from all angles of the wood; it was uplifting and soothing. I made my way back through a field of long grasses that mingled with tall daisies, their bright, cushioned centres reflecting the sun. The sweet-smelling clover brushed my nostrils and stayed with me for many days. Several white butterflies chased past, adding to the perfection of the day. Then, for a few moments, I went back to my childhood. I sat and made a daisy chain.

I reluctantly walked back to the grime of the town, to the annoying task of having to queue at some ghastly checkout for a few commodities that I needed. I pitied the many people who hurried along, high heels tapping a frantic rhythm on the pavements. Sorry for the ones that had never wandered through a field infused with poppies. Never smelt the clover or the scent of wild honeysuckle after rain. As children, did they ever skim stones over a stream or pond? And, know the childish joy of your rock out beating your friends?

I've lived in a time when all these things have been possible and if we make more people aware of the countryside and its beauty around us. Suppose we can stem the tide of pollution. But we are slowly ruining the planet and are drifting on a course to nowhere.

* * *

A Childhood Memory

I was seven years old and on holiday with my parents, brother, and sisters in Rochester, Kent, when I was ill. I had awoken that morning complaining of a bad headache and feeling sick. As it had been a hot day before, my Mother thought it was a case of too much sun. She gave me aspirin. I drank lots of water. I remember her sponging my face with cold water to cool me down. I had to stay in bed during that night. I was terribly sick and very restless and cried to go home, being no better in the morning. My parents decided to return home to Portsmouth. I slept through the journey and was sick again when I awoke. I also had an earache and suffered blurred vision. My father carried me home from the station. I was not well enough now to walk.

My mother was frantic with worry and called in a neighbour called Mrs. Knee, a member of The Red Cross. She took my temperature and told my mother I was seriously ill. I was wrapped in a blanket and immediately taken to Portsmouth General Hospital. A mastoid operation was performed on me within hours of my arrival.

In those days (over forty years ago), a mastoid operation was considered a major operation. My parents told me that over a few days, I hovered between life and death. I was so ill that I was in a room, and my parents were allowed to visit me at all hours. Sometimes, I was conscious and could not see correctly, and I remember feeling lonely in this little, very quiet room all on my own. A kindly woman flitted in and out, and one day, I asked her if I would die. Because I was all alone and cut off by myself.

"No, Dear." she replied." You are nearly well enough to be with the other children".
The day at last had arrived when I was on the ward with the rest of the children, sight fully restored but head still swathed in bandages (I had the feeling of two heads on my small shoulders). It was lovely being with the other children, and I soon made friends with a little girl in the bed next to me. We shared sweets and comics.

I loved visiting hours, and my mother would bring me digestive biscuits; they were and still are my favourites. I used to keep them on a green tin in my locker; a rather greedy nurse used to help herself to them. They must have been her favourite biscuits too.

I did not like the food in the hospital: the eggs were always challenging, the porridge looked like wallpaper paste, and cabbage, which I detested, was served daily.
One day, we had stewed apples, and I told the nurses that I had a locust in mine; of course, it was a clove, but it did cause a laugh. On another occasion, I told Mother. "We had soup with horrible pimples in it." It was pearl barley. To this day, I call pearl barley 'pimples.'

I was in the hospital for several weeks, and now I wanted to go home. My little friend in the next bed to me had left the hospital, and there was a horrid little girl in her place who kept sticking her tongue out at me. I was unhappy and wanted to go home to my cosy little bed. This iron bedstead was hard and uncomfortable; the pillows felt like rock and did nothing to help the constant ache in my head.

One day, at long last, the bandages were removed from my head for the last time how lightheaded I felt. I put my hand up behind my ear and touched the deep scar. I shuddered at the feel of it, and when I looked in the mirror, I started to cry as my hair from one side had been cut off. The nurse kindly explained this was necessary and reassured me that my hair would soon grow again.

A few days after having the bandages removed, I was told I was going home. Although I had lost a lot of weight and was now very thin, the doctor thought I was well enough to be discharged. Our kind neighbour, Mrs. Knee, called to collect me in her car along with Mother and my sister. I kissed my favourite nurse goodbye and stepped out into the fresh air. How good it felt to be going home.

By Jussie E. Lilliot

The tutor who marked this piece remarked.

"I thought this was your best piece yet. Written and convincingly told".

* * *

The Wall or Henry's Wall

The cottage was in the triangle of a hill right in the corner. The garden wall was built of Cotswold Stone. Here, Henry would sit for hours, passing the time of day with people from all walks of life. He suffered cruelly from Asthma and had to retire early from work. His garden was his life. The aubretia would cascade like a purple waterfall from the wall crevices in the spring. In the field beyond, splashes of red poppies would remind Henry of his two brothers lost in battle at Flanders.

Henry could be seen pottering about in his garden, but even small tasks like a little hoeing or weeding would leave him breathless, and he would have to rest before continuing any further. But despite his laboured breathing, he enjoyed life and a joke. like the day when one of the locals told Henry he overheard one of the villagers, the vicar's wife, and her son drinking in the pub, and they had just opened. Her frosty reply was,
    "Yes, I know, and if I could spare the time, I would join him."
Both men laughed raucously. Then Henry would relate the story of how he and his four brothers had arranged to have their photographs taken. They had donned their best suits and turned up for their appointment with no hair out of place. The photographer remarked on the five immaculate, handsome men. He went to great lengths and spent a lot of time lining them up to get the best picture possible. He then disappeared under a tunnel of black cloth and was about to take their photograph when one of them broke wind, loud and long. They doubled up with joy and could not control their laughter. Consequently, the photograph was never taken. The photographer barred them from his premises and then told the story to every photographer in the area.

Hilda was Henry's wife. A pretty woman with fair wavy hair now streaked with threads of silver. Her skin was clear and unlined. She had solemn brown eyes which glowed when she looked at Henry. Hilda was blessed with an inner strength that could see her through any life crisis. She would make numerous pots of strong dark tea and join Henry by the wall. George, the gardener who worked at the big house opposite, would often join Henry for a mug of tea. Henry would raise the large enamel mug to him, signaling that tea was brewed. George would give him the thumbs up, meaning the master was out, and come clambering over the wall.

Over tea, the two men would discuss who would win at the races that day. Henry would ask George to put a shilling each way on a certain horse, not a word to Hilda. She frowned upon such things as gambling. If the horse lost the race, he would solemnly cuss it and declare "no more betting" until next week. They would drain the last of the tea from Hilda's giant brown teapot, and then George would quickly exit back over the wall before his masters returned. Every Autumn, George picked bowls of sloes from the abundant bushes in the area and would toss a bag full over the wall for Henry to make sloe wine with. Henry relished the heartwarming drink on a cold winter's day.

Hilda was artful, and she kept it in the cellar. After each tot, she marked it with a pencil, but Henry grew wise to this, and when she went to her church meetings, he would sip the sloe wine and top it up to the mark with water. Hilda was none the wiser but remarked that the wine did seem to lose its strength the longer it was kept.

The potato peelings, bacon rinds, stale crusts, and vegetable matter were collected in an old tin bucket and sent over the wall to the big house. This was mulched down and added to the chicken food. In exchange, back over the wall came a basketful of large eggs. Some of these were preserved in icing glass for the days when the hens weren't laying very well. Often, a brace of pheasants would be found down by the wall after a shoot. Whoever left them knew they would be appreciated. Rabbits were plentiful and cheap, Hilda made delicious pies and nourishing stews from them, and the roast rabbit was often on the menu for Sunday. Nothing was wasted. Henry made a good pair of slippers from the skins. He sat under the old apple tree to read the daily paper. Here, the sunlight dappled sunlight filtered through and fell upon his sinewy arms. Arms that once had been strong and held babies and loved ones.

Henry sauntered over to the wall; he knew the time of day by the old road sweeper. His ruddy, weather-beaten face with the stubble chin was always a welcome sight. Yes, right on time, as usual. He wore his battered brown cap and brown corded trousers tied with string under the knees.

"Ow be today the Henry, nice drop o' rain we 'ad, just right for me tayties." Hilda would come out with steaming mugs of her strong dark tea for the men. She was happy when Henry had someone to chat to over the wall. The old road sweeper thanked Hilda and went on his way, gnarled hands pushing his barrow.

Henry would sit on the wall until dark, watching the sun slip from its scarlet hue into the purple dusk. He often saw a wonderful v formation of ducks approaching the river in the late evening. Their wings whirred gently in *the still quiet air. A nightingale could often be heard in the old apple tree. Hidden from man's gaze, its beautiful, uplifting song in the cool of the day was very healing.*

Autumn arrived with its rich harvest pickings. Hilda loved the soft gold of September morning. It took her back to her childhood in Kent, when, as a child, she would help her mother take jugs of cool lemonade down to the harvesters in the field beyond their farmhouse. She could still remember the heady smell of hops. Her mother's jam-making session would last several weeks and consist of plum, plum, apple, blackberry and apple, apple jelly, and damson.

Down by Henry's wall, the apple tree bore the delicious Blenheim Orange. Hilda would sell these for sixpence per pound. This extra income gave them a pile of logs to see through the cold winter months. The log man(as Hilda called him)called regular every Saturday, and for one shilling, you could get a sackful. But this year, the money would be going to a different cause. Hilda needed a new set of false teeth, but there was never enough money to spare for such vanities. So she prayed for a good crop, and her prayers were answered. It was a bounteous season, the boughs heavy with apples, almost to breaking point. Off Hilda went into town and came home smiling from ear to ear, new teeth dazzling Henry. She always referred to them as "her apple teeth." Henry was sad to see autumn depart, her glorious mantle of colour with her. It was a typical November day. The mist dripped from the surrounding trees, throwing a thin grey veil over the cottage and garden. Henry would sit by a comforting log fire on days like these, listening to the wireless. There was no television in those far-off days. Visitors were few in those winter months, but George from the big house opposite would endeavour a call. George was never surprised to find Henry with a cloth over his head, leaning over a bowl and inhaling Friars Balsam. This method helped to make his breathing easier. Despondency was never far away from Henry when winter showed its dreaded face.

Gusts of violent winds rattled on the windowpanes and found their way into the cottage through every conceivable gap. Hilda served bowls of hot, nourishing porridge to start the day with. For dinner at midday, a hearty stew made from scrag ends with herbs and dumplings added. Baked liver on a bed of onions or a mouth-watering steak and kidney pudding, simmering away on the black range for most of the morning in a large basin topped by a pudding cloth. A jug of piping hot cocoa would be made before Henry climbed the wooden hill(his term for stairs).

An ordinary house brick was put in the oven to get hot. It was then wrapped in a piece of flannel and put in the bed, where it would keep hot for several hours.

In the inky blackness of the night, an owl hooted in the apple tree. Its haunting, ghostly, quivering hoot repeated many times. Henry drew the curtains and shut out the winter night.

Henry woke and peered out of the window. The landscape looked barren, and the leafless boughs stood against the sky. The starlings were pecking at the iron-hard earth in their search for food. On the wall was a line of sparrows or spadgers, as Henry called them, their feathers fluffed out like capes around them for warmth. Above, crows circled in large numbers over the bleak and frosty fields. Henry longed for spring when he could sit by the wall again. He slowly made his way downstairs and sat by a roaring fire.

George called to see Henry that morning and bought him a small bottle of Henry's favourite tipple. George sat warming his hands by the fire. "You are in the best place this morning, Henry; brass monkey weather outside." Hilda reached for the large mug, filled it to the brim with scalding hot tea, and passed it to George. He sat there, hands cupped around the mug, enjoying his tea and fire. George was reluctant to leave their warm hospitality, but jobs were waiting for him at the big house. Hilda saw him at the door and thanked him for calling and for the tonic(tipple). She closed the door and drew the heavy green velvet curtain across, making the room warm, cosy, and chill-proof. That was the last time either of them saw George.

The following day, George cycled out of the drive as he had done a dozen times before. But this time, he had made the fatal mistake of not looking in both directions before moving out into the road. He went straight into the path of an oncoming car and died instantly.

It was a black day for Henry. His asthma worsened, he took to his bed, and there he stayed for several days. Henry felt complete desolation of spirit. He would miss George with his happy, friendly face and toothy grin. George had been a staunch friend to Hilda and himself. These were anxious days for her; she cosseted him and was patient and kind. She drew upon her inner strength. The district nurse was called every day. She was a jolly buxom lady with a kind disposition. Henry stated she always called at the wrong time of day for him. He was either listening to the racing results or wanting to sleep. But Hilda supposed it was because he didn't want a blanket bath.

"I don't want nurses fussing over me," he would say. Nevertheless, the nurse insisted on the blanket bath. Henry's strength slowly returned, and he went downstairs to sit by the crackling log fire. Henry and Hilda discussed the day George died over a pot of soothing tea. Henry described it" as the day God called for George."

It started to snow, tiny flakes merging into larger flakes that tumbled out of leaden skies and fell softly to the ground. A blanket of snow covered the garden, and everywhere looked bleak and bare. During the night, the snow billowed against Henry's wall; it lodged for several days. Dark storm clouds scuttled across the wintry skies. Henry was dispirited and reluctant to leave his bed during these bitterly cold days. The winter was long, icy, and grey.

Then came that wonderful time when winter melted into spring. Henry took a stroll into the garden and looked over the wall. There was a chill in the air, but all the signs of spring were there. The aubretia was about to burst forth, the daffodils were trying to shed their coverings of green, and the birds in the apple tree were greeting spring's renewal with their sweet song. Hilda watched Henry walking up the garden path. Her heart ached; he looked weary and ashen. The long dreary winter had taken its toll. The shock of George's death was still with them both. She knew how fervently Henry longed for the sun's warmth and how he drew strength from it. He was eager to chat with new and old faces over the wall. Hilda knew it was just a question of time; she hoped he would be spared to enjoy the so long for summer, but it was not to be. His breathing was shallow, and the pump for his asthma was in constant use. He took to the warmth of his bed. Downstairs, Hilda sat alone by the dying red embers of the fire and wept. It had been a long and happy marriage. She went upstairs to see him. He asked her to draw the curtains aside. The moon shone bright in a velvet sky. In the early hours of the morning, Henry passed away. Peacefully and quietly in his sleep. The asthma attacks had weakened his heart, and all his strength had left him. No more would he hear the nightingale in the apple tree.

* * *

As A Wall

A (broken wall) almost buried in nettles, that's all left of me now. Once, I was solid and supportive, but now, when the wind moans over me, a little more of the cement loosens and crumbles into dust. Bricks that were new and sad are now faded and worn (with age). Even the ivy that clad me and clung tight has wrapped itself around the gnarled oak tree adjacent to me.

A grey lizard will come wriggling out of the holes to bask in the sunshine and dart away into the undergrowth. Last night, an old tramp sought refuge and rested at the bottom of me, covering himself with layers of newspapers to ward off the early autumn chill. I heard him sighing and gasping in his sleep. When he woke, he ate a breakfast of blackberries that sprawled alongside. No one who came this way could visit those jewel-like fruits glistening in the sun.

In my prime, sweethearts have sat down by me, people have picnicked and spread me with colourful cloth, and their children have used me for a seat and have dug their heels into my sides. Once, a little girl with a polka-dot ribbon sat with long legs dangling, reciting Humpty Dumpty. I have often given rest to a weary traveller out on long walks and have been involved in games of hide and seek. Only last summer, a wren built its tiny nest in one of the notches. I do hope he will return next spring. A Painted Lady or a Red Admiral would often stay awhile, fragile wings opening and shutting with the most delicate movements. Many a snail has crawled along me and left its tell trail sign, a thin tracery line like a silver seam. Some were unfortunate to be spotted by the eyes of a beady blackbird whose yellow beak could be merciless!

A big cat that used to sit on me and stretch completely out on a sunny day would watch and pounce on an unsuspecting mouse or bird in the long grass. Then, ginger fur and feathers would fly in all directions. I never see him these days; perhaps, like me, his best days are over! Winter has come and gone. The snow billowed against me and lodged for several days before evaporating while the relentless gales tore at my foundations. But I'm still here defying the elements. That is all that is left of me.

By Jussie E. Lilliot

Chapter 5

The telephone rang. It was Mum telling me that Aunty Betty had just phoned her to say, Julie, her daughter, had decided to drive to Ash, Kent, to find Sheerwater Farm, The Grove Ferry, and to go and visit the churches and the church parishes and to find out more about our family history. Mum was invited to join them. Julie could take a few days off work in a few months, and Mum could sort out a few days' holiday from her reception job. She would be taking some of the old photos with her to compare how different the places would look today from yesteryear, especially Sheerwater Farm and The Grove Jetty.
It was a great idea, as it was apparent by now that Mum wouldn't receive any replies to the letters she had sent.

But I was wrong!

In the post the following morning, Mum had finally received some responses to her inquiries.

"You wait ages for one bus to turn up, then they all turn up at once!" said Mum, overwhelmed.

The first letter Mum opened was sincerely written and signed by Marie Rootes, who lived at Sheerwater Farm, Ash, Canterbury, Kent.

Dear Mrs Warne,

Thank you for your letter, sorry for the delay— we've had visitors from Canada and it's put me all behind!

I have spoken to Mrs Doreen Fagg. She'll give you what help she can; please contact her directly.

Good Hunting.

And she left a forwarding address to Doreen Fagg.

Mum wrote back straight away to Doreen and hoped she wouldn't have to wait too long for a reply. She hoped to meet up with these people and arrange something when she visited Ash with her sister and niece. Mum also replied to Marie from Sheerwater Farm, thanking her immensely and adding that she would be visiting the area soon with her sister and niece and asked if she would mind if they could make a fleeting visit along the way and see where their dear Mother had been born.

The second letter Mum opened was from Western Australia - a family historian - wrote a letter.

Dear Joyce,

My humble apologies for the delay in attending to your request. I have put off trying to contact your cousins due to other pressing matters to do with our society.

This afternoon, I had your letter come to the top of the heap and thought I had better do something about it. I started by writing one letter with the thought of photocopying several to send out, went to address some envelopes, and realised there were some LEAVER addresses within a low-charge zone to telephone. I dialled one number and got an answer. It was the wife of one of your cousins, the terrible thing about it is that he died last Friday. I feel very bad about this, but I am sorry it happened through my neglect in doing something for you before this.

However, the other brother was there and both the widow and brother got on the phone and heard about the inquiry; they wanted your name and address, so I am sending letters to them in this mail.

Mr. Harry LEAVER, Port Denison Western Australia
Mrs. F.L. LEAVER, Tooday, Western Australia

I did not ask Mrs. Leaver what her name was, but checking on the Electoral Roll, I see her name is Annie Morcombe LEAVER. Her husband was Frank LILLIOT LEAVER. So there you have it, the LILLIOT being given to a son!

As my costs have been very small, I am returning some of the stamps you sent.

All best wishes, I trust you have pleasure in this contact; next thing you will be hopping onto a plane to come out and visit! It has given me pleasure to be able to assist you in your search.

Yours sincerely,
Alan Campbell

Mum and her sisters were overjoyed and shocked that Mum had received this letter.

"Well, Out of all the people in Australia, our cousin has been found that easy. It's such a shame, though, that the elder son had just passed away the week prior."

It was indeed remarkable. All Mum had done was write a letter to the address from the back of the black and white bungalow sent to her Mother in 1948. The family living there now must have forwarded Mum's letter to a local historian. The sisters and Mum immediately wrote to Harry and Frank's widow, Annie. Soon after, Mum received a large padded brown envelope with much family tree history. Also attached was a letter from Doreen Fagg.

Dear Mrs. Warne,

Many thanks for your letter concerning the "Lilliot family." As you can see by the enclosed letter, I passed it on to Nan Barlow, who is my father's first cousin, making Joseph Lilliot my great-grandfather. If you come and visit Nan when you visit the area, I'm sure the tongues will do overtime!

Yours sincerely,
Doreen Fagg

Enclosed was a letter from Nan Barlow, a distant cousin. She was also the same lady in the photos in the box at Gran's house, one holding a baby and standing next to Ruth (Who was possibly Gran's sister) in the other photograph.

Dear Mrs. Warne,

Mrs. Fagg has passed your letter on to me, being an earlier generation perhaps I could be a little more helpful remembering tales my father used to love to tell.

I am now 85, my mother was Helen Lilliott before she married, the 2nd daughter of Joseph Lilliott and your Grandfather was his brother" Uncle Tom" as even I used to know him. I am very sorry I cannot tell you where your mother was married; probably she wasn't, when the chronicles were written. Your grandparents were married at Sandwich. I knew your aunt "Annie Lilliot". I remember going in my early teens with my mother to Marshside when your aunt had just gotten married. I also knew Sid Lilliot; he used to visit my mother sometimes, in fact, I attended his funeral at Ash a few years ago.

The reason for the Lilliott Chronicle to be discontinued was the simple fact that the writer and composer died, his death was about 1910/1912, and it was of course your grandfather's other brother Edward, a cripple from birth.

I suppose no one else had the inclination, time or inspiration to follow suit. I remember him well, he used to come over from Sandwich to Grove Corner when all Joseph's offspring would meet for the day. (lovely memories) at Christmas. I must tell you that your Grandmother was a fond favourite with my mother. She used to call her "Aunt Sally" and I believe she was a very smart lady. I never met her myself, but one hears these tales, and by my dear mother's version, in fact, she was the one who helped me into the world!!

I imagine my father and mother took Sheerwater Farm when your grandparents left. I heard I was one year old when we went there.

I am sorry I cannot remember anything about your mother. Perhaps if you are coming this way shortly, I shall be pleased to have a chat with you. I knew your Grandfather as "Uncle Tom" and during the First World War at any rate, he worked for my Grandfather (Joseph) at Grove, and he lived then at Upstreet.

Perhaps you could give me a ring before you visit me, so that I can be sure to be in.
(She left her telephone number, and underneath wrote).

Hope you can understand this rigmarole of memories,

Yours sincerely,

Nan Barlow.

In the envelope among Nan Barlow and Doreen Fagg's letters was a poem by Helen Griggs. At the top was Nan Barlow's handwriting: Poems composed by Nan Barlow's Mother. At least Mum could start to fathom out who belonged to whom in this intriguing family tree of hers.

GOD PLANTED A GARDEN EASTWARD IN ZION

Our lives are gardens planned by God
The gardens of the soul
Wherein is sown some precious seed
And we are in control.
Firstly we need the cleansing power
The soil is full of sin,
If we accept the Saviour's love
His cleansing then flows in.

Our implements of faith and hope
Will help to clear the ground,
For weeds and rubbish quickly grow
And briars may be found.

The fertilising gift of prayer
Will feed the hungry soul,
While showers of blessing from above
Will purify the whole.

What flowers should in our garden bloom?
Pure lilies there must be.
The Bible says the pure in heart
Their God shall surely see.

Heartsease and pansies must unite
In thoughtful care and grace
To help the sick and lonely ones
And show a smiling face.

*The lowly violet, sweet and rich
In living kindness still
And seek to do God's will.*

*Pale primrose, coming in the Spring,
Hard Winter may have borne,
Now it can help the weaker ones
And comfort those who mourn.*

*Night-scented stock will play its part,
Though most times out of sight,
Its perfume rising high to cheer
Long watches of the night.*

*We'll not forget the best of all,
Sweet-scented rose of love,
It scatters incense all around
In praise to God above.*

*The rambler climbing o'er the wall
To see its brothers need
Can help the homeless in despair,
Also the hunger feed.*

*More flowers could in my garden grow,
I know there's room to spare
I try and do my very best,
God knows what blossoms there.*

*Listen, 'tis eventide,
I hear a soft and pleasing sound
Like fragrant breezes on the air,
The Master walks around.*

*He's come to call the workmen home,
And to review his land,
Unworthy, yes, but all is well. The Master takes his hand-*

And leads him to a brighter realm,

Promotion, high above,
Where now he'll serve his Master
In the perfect garden– LOVE

HELEN GRIGGS

Mum loved the poem. She had found it quite surprising that her Great Aunt Helen Griggs writings were on the same par and very similar to the way mum thought and wrote too. Reading the poem influenced and encouraged Mum to further her creative writing course at college, to widen it and approach poetry writing. She had already won a Valentine's poetry competition, which had boosted her confidence.

Also in the envelope, Nan had written across the top of the paged article: Spring 1972 extract from Kent Journal of the Association of Men of Kent and Kentish men. There was a photo of three rather elegant-looking ladies, with a headline from the article reading:

THREE LITTLE MAIDS FROM KENT ARE WE…
Ninety, ninety-two and three.

Close to 100 years ago– in December 1873, to be exact – a young farmer from Westmarsh, an isolated parish near Ash-next-Sandwich, married a girl from Deal and took his bride to his farm.
 He was Joseph Lilliott, then just 23, and an early photograph shows him to have been a handsome young man with a splendid beard and fine, penetrating, but kindly blue eyes. His wife was Helen Cox Culmer, from her name, a member of a family anciently settled in East Kent.
 Joseph's father, Edward, had come from Westerham, and he was the son of Thomas Lilliott, born in 1778 of a family believed to be of Huguenot stock.
 One evening recently one of Joseph's daughters, Helen, talked to me in her cosy home. Whytegates, on The Forstal, Preston, near Canterbury. Helen, or to give her respect, which is her due. Mrs. George Griggs is now aged 93, and she has two younger sisters who are only 92 and 90. They are Mrs. Edmund Griggs (Rose) of Preston and Mrs. Edwin Knight (Ethel) of Littlebourne.

With blue eyes shining like her father Joseph's, Mrs Griggs recaptured for me some recollections of the past, related with a soft Kent burr that gently overlays a voice of innate culture.

'They used to say my grandfather came down to this part of Kent carrying all his possessions in a red handkerchief on a stick,' she said with a smile.' I don't know how true this is, but times were certainly hard."

"My brother Alfred and myself were born in Westmarsh, but when I was a year old, we moved to Grove, and my father took Hook Farm, which used to be known as Grove Corner Farm. There, my sisters were born."

To the Forefront

The name of Alfred Lilliott was to become one of the best-known in the farming world of East Kent. Magistrate. Rural District Councillor, Parish Councillor, and Poor Law Guardian he was at the forefront of all local activities, and two of his sons still farm in the district. But this is to digress, for his sister Helen continues the story.

"We all lived at Grove until we married, and we went to the school at Preston. It was a two-mile walk, so we had to take our lunch with us, and I remember sitting and eating it around the circular iron stove in the schoolroom. It was a Church of England School, and one day, the vicar, who was a retired bishop – Bishop Jenner – gave me a catechism book. But we were strict about "Chapel," when my father saw it, he put it on the highest cupboard out of reach.'

Mrs Griggs is a gifted artist. Her paintings of flowers on plates and her oil landscapes are well known in East Kent, and one of her proud possessions is a beautiful Scottish scene painted on a plate. This won her a prize for painting "Over Sixties." I asked her if she had received lessons. "No, I'm self-taught," she answered. 'My father was told I should go to a School of Art, but of course, he could not afford that. It would have meant going to Grove Ferry station and travelling by train to Canterbury. "The only brush for you is a scrubbing brush." he told me.

"When we were young, there was no Post Office at Preston, and the postman used to walk from Sturry five miles away, and when he got to Grove, he would blow a horn, and we would have to go and collect the letters. Then, he would get some odd jobs of shoe mending to do for the day and blow his horn to collect any letters before returning to Sturry. To get to a Post Office for a Savings Bank meant going to Grove Ferry and travelling into Canterbury by train.'

'We only went into Canterbury once a year. This was at Michaelmas when we would buy our clothes for the next twelve months. My mother would buy unbleached Calico and have it made up into nightdresses for us girls—and it was pretty rough, I can tell you.

"We all used to work on the farm. My father used to pay us a penny a gallon for picking black currants and raspberries. But then, if he had a good harvest, perhaps he would give us £5 – which was great riches. In wintertime, there was skating on the icy marshes. When I married, I went with my husband to Sheerwater Farm, near Ash. It was a struggle in those days. I used to get up as soon as it was light and go into the fields to pick strawberries. No rubber boots in those days, and our feet just got wet. The strawberries went to Covent Garden from Adisham or Grove Ferry, and we were paid 6d. for a gallon—seven pounds.'

"Strawberry teas were a great event in the year. There would be a service in the barn for which I learned t to play the organ. Then, everyone would be served with their strawberry teas. Once, we had a visiting preacher who went on and on and then complained that we sang the hymns too fast. Today, they say hymns aren't sung fast enough."

Opposite The Lilliotts Farm was the Knights Farmhouse, and the children from both families played together and went to school together. From the Knight family, Ethel found her sweetheart and became Mrs Ethel Knight. Helen and Rose married two brothers from the large family of Griggs from Preston. So, the families became linked with 'farming' families in the area.

Mrs Griggs is not only an accomplished painter but also a musician. For over 40 years, she was an organist at the pretty little Congregational Chapel.

She has taken an active part in all village life, as have her sisters Rose and Ethel. Their families have grown up and married, and each of them retains as vital an interest in the present as in the past. Ethel was a Methodist lay preacher for many years; Rose taught in a Sunday School at Preston for a long period.

Perhaps they sometimes sigh for the serenity of the past despite its hardships. This part of Kent is their world; they have helped to make it and would like to preserve it from the onrush of modernisation. Maybe too many urban dwellers have sought 'olde world' cottages in Kent without knowing too well the story of its past and the character of the people who have made it—like Helen, Rose, and Ethel Lilliott. - A. R.

At the bottom of the page was a faded black and white photo of the three sisters beside a large fireplace. The caption next to them: *Mrs Helen Griggs (standing), with the painted plate which won her first place in an over-60s contest, Mrs Rose Griggs(centre), and Mrs Ethel Knight, pictured at Whyte gates on April 1.*

Mum smiled at the article. Mavis, her sister, also played an active part in the local church, St. Mary's in Kintbury. Mum liked the idea of painting on a plate, which she had never tried before, let alone paint, but she could only try.

"Mmm", she thought. "Poetry and painting, why not?

Mum was amazed by the knowledge and history coming her way and to think that her Mother's family was still alive and had stayed in rural Kent.

The next article was also a photocopy from a paper - *The Christian Herald and The Signs of Our Times,* dated October 13, 1979.

Four hundred years ago, another kind of "boat people" - Huguenots from Flanders and France – flooded into South-Eastern England in an attempt to escape persecution at home. Among the most notable of these refugees was Deryk Carver, who says JOHN WRIGHT, died for his Protestant faith at the head of a . . .

Noble Army of Martyrs.

"The inhabitants of the coast were thrown into a state of commotion by the sudden arrival of many destitute French people from the opposite coast. Some came in open boats, others in sailing vessels. They were of all classes and conditions, and among them were women and children.

"Some crossed the Channel in midwinter, during the stormiest weather, and when they reached the English shore, they usually fell upon their knees and thanked God for their deliverance."

Samuel Smiles was writing of the "boat people" of over 400 years ago, the Huguenots, who flooded into south-eastern England as refugees, Protestants fleeing from religious persecution in Flanders and France. They came in such numbers that they are said to have trebled the population of Canterbury. At Rye, in Sussex, there were 641 refugees within three days of the Massacre of St Bartholomew (1572), and in the next ten years, their number in this then-

important seaport was almost 2,000. The Mayor issued an order forbidding any more "unless merchants, gents, poste messengers, or the like."

It is no wonder that at one time, there were up to 30 French churches in England, mostly in eastern and southern parts. Today, there are three survivors with regular services in the French language.

One is, naturally, in London—in Soho Square; a second, by ancient royal decree, is in the Chapel of the Black Prince, in the crypt of Canterbury Cathedral. It should be remembered that not only was Canterbury full of Huguenots in Elizabeth's reign, but that firm protagonist of the Protestant cause in France, Odet de Coligny, brother of the Admiral, died at Canterbury, most likely of poison, and was buried in the cathedral.

The third is at Brighton, where there has been French preaching continuously from the 16th century and where the French Protestant Church has for nearly a century had its own chapel, built in the 1880s with much financial help from the Reformed Evangelical Church in France.

It is customary to say that the Huguenot cause in Brighton began with Deryk (the name has several spellings) Carver. There were, however, probably already French fisherfolk settlers in the fishing village of Brighthelmstone before Carver and his family were chased out of Flanders about 1546. He was a "predicant." a lay preacher in our terminology. At his house of the Black Lion of Flanders, services of prayer and Bible reading were held regularly and attracted not only the French immigrants but also ardent English Protestants, for Carver immediately set about acquiring English to take advantage of the decree of Edward VI's reign allowing the use of the vernacular in worship.

One day in October 1554, with Mary on the throne, the county magistrate and his troop descended on Carver's meeting place and arrested him and 11 others who were "in their prayers and saying the service in English." They were flung into jail at Newgate and lay there for eight or nine months awaiting trial.

Carver took advantage of his detention to improve his command of English. The keeper testified to this and his progress." although he (Carver) was well stricken in years, past the time of learning" he was 40!
The use of the vernacular was an important point with Carver, who wrote in his "confession." that he was "honest as a Huguenot." as the saying was, he

refused to recant: "There is no salvation for a Christian man, except it should be said in the mother tongue that he might understand it."

Speaking in English, Carver did not mince his words at his trial before Edmund Bonner, Bishop of London: "If Christ was here, you would put Him to a worse death than He was put to before."

On July 22, 1555, in the centre of Lewes, the county town of Sussex, before the sign of the star, Deryk Carver went to the stake. His English Bible was thrown into the barrel of pitch so that it should be burnt, too. He stepped in, picked it out, and threw it to the crowd, and although the Sheriff ordered it to be thrown back in the Queen's name, it most likely never was.

As the flames wrapped around him, he exclaimed: "Lord, Thou has written that he will not forsake wife, children, house, and all that he hath and take up Thy Cross and follow Thee, is not worthy of Thee. But Thou knowest, Lord, that I have forsaken all to follow Thee." And he had, for he was a family man with considerable wealth.

The Carver household remained true to their father's confession and on their property in the old town of Brighton, the Huguenot service seems to have continued after Carver's death. Close by is Union Street, denoting in its name the link between the English and French Protestants, and here stands a chapel (now Elim Pentecostalism), which through the centuries was variously termed "Presbyterian "and "Independent."

The present building goes back to Brighton Regency days. Still, it contains parts (particularly the east wall of Sussex Flint in Meeting House Lane) belonging to its predecessor built in 1689 when a new wave of French Protestants flocked over the Channel following the Revocation of the Edict of Nantes (1685)and the English Protestants were just beginning to feel the easing of pressure which came with the Toleration Act.

There were three faded photos in the article. One was a photo of the Martyrs Memorial at Lewes, Sussex, which noted that "The name "Diricke" Carver heads the list of 17 people burnt at the stake at this spot."

The next was of the Entrance to the Black Prince Chapel in the crypt of Canterbury Cathedral, where a French service has been held regularly for centuries. The last photo showed a French Protestant Church, off Regency Square, Brighton, one of only three places in Britain where French services are still held.

Mum then opened another handwritten envelope; it simply read *Grove Ferry*. Inside were two snippets taken from a newspaper, one an old photo of the ferryman with his water vessel amongst people waiting to board. The typed writing underneath read, "Grove Ferry around the turn of the century– The photograph is being used on the poster for Saturday's postcard fair, which is in the St Peters Street Methodist Church Hall.

The second newspaper snippet was a modern-day photo cutting from the area's local newspaper.

RELAX AT THE GROVE FERRY INN

As the water rat observed in The Wind in the Willows. "There is nothing- absolutely nothing -half as much fun as messing about on the water." And where better to do it than in the picture postcard setting of the Grove Ferry Inn, nestling high on the banks of the River Stour at Upstreet?

Built-in 1832 on the site of an old coaching inn, it has long enjoyed a reputation as one of Kent's most attractive pubs, a haven for peace and relaxation in an often hectic and noisy world.

Bought nearly four years ago by Mr. John Mitchell, the inn has recently been refurbished to provide all the comforts of modern-day living without detracting from the character of the original building.

"A substantial amount of money, time, and effort has been spent making the Grove Ferry Inn a place where people can relax and enjoy the riverside atmosphere." Said manager Mr David Huntley.

"Where else can one enjoy a leisurely stroll along the picturesque river and a drink or a meal at one of the county's oldest pubs?" The inn, offering an extensive menu, is fast becoming one of the area's most popular eating places. Take your pick from a selection of four roast meats in the Carvery; enjoy a succulent steak cooked to your exact specifications, or choose from the cold buffet.

And don't forget chef Paolo de Paoli's chef's specials-the results of years of experience working abroad. And with the introduction of a children's menu and family room with a play area, the Grove Ferry Inn now welcomes family groups with open arms.

"We'd like to think that we have something for everybody at a price everybody can afford, "said Mr Huntley. Recent changes to restaurant licensing laws mean the Grove Ferry Inn is now open every afternoon, seven days a week, making it an ideal place to make that business meeting. Bookings for afternoon meals can be made with Mr Huntley's team of friendly staff on Chislet 302. With two bars, the family room, the riverside terrace, and a beer garden. And with a large car park, you won't have to worry about overcrowding or finding somewhere to park your car. Why not see for yourself. Just follow the signs from the A28 Margate Road in Upstreet. See you there!

The article included a photo of the pub, taken from across the river.

Mum was enjoying all this information unfolding around here. She had to stop and have a cup of tea and a pause. Never had she ever imagined that by writing a few letters to random addresses, any of this history would still be around. It was exciting news. She couldn't wait to read what else was in the large envelope In front of her and share it with the rest of her family.

Next were some historical papers from The Lilliott Family.

Lilliott Chronological Record

Edward Lilliott began this in 1811. As previous records were unavailable, Elizabeth Lilliott stated that she remembered her Grandfather, Lilliott. He appears to have lived in Westerham. It is said that he ended his days with his married daughter, Mrs. Day, at Upper Norwood. And was buried in the parish churchyard.

The most notable person of the whole is Edward Lilliott, a senior who, by his marriage, saved the family from extinction.

The Lilliotts came over from France with the Huguenots and settled in Sandwich.

There are several families of Lilliots in Brittany today. We hope to find out more.

This was attached to an extremely old, worn document of Edwards' will.

Lilliott Chronological Record

Edward Lilliott began this in 1811. As previous records are not available Elizabeth Lilliott stated that she remembered her grandfather Lilliott. He appears to have lived at Westerham. It is said that he ended his days with his married daughter Mrs Day at upper Norwood and was buried in the parish churchyard.

The most notable person of the whole is Edward Lilliott Senior who by his marriage he saved the family from extinction.

The Lilliotts came over from France with the Huguenots and settled in Sandwich.

There are several families of Lilliots in Brittany today - we hope to find out more.

OFFICE COPY
VALID ONLY IF BEARING
IMPRESS OF COURT SEAL

I Edward Lillott of Westmarsh in the Parish of Ash-next-Sandwich do hereby revoke all former Wills and Testaments and do make this my last Will and Testament and I hereby direct my dear Wife as Executrix and my two Sons Edward Lillott and Joseph Lillott as Executors and Trustees of this my Will as soon as may be after my decease to pay all my just debts and I authorize my said Wife Jane Lillott and my two sons aforesaid to carry on my business of Farmer and Market Gardener at Westmarsh in the Parish of Ash next Sandwich and for that purpose to continue the occupation of the House Premises and Land used by me at my decease and to employ in the said business such portions of my personal estate as she may think fit and I empower my said Executrix and Trustees to manage my present estate generally in such a manner as shall appear to them to be most advantageous to my family investing the surplies in their names and varying the investments as they shall think fit And I hereby give my said Wife all the income from the said business as well as any interest or rents arising from any real or personal estate possessed by me at my decease Nevertheless charged with the maintenance education and bringing up in a manner suitable to their station of life of my Sons until they attain the age of twenty one years and of my Daughters until they marry And in the event of my wife marrying again I dissannul the powers and bequests here before given to her and give her absolutely all my household effects linen books plate &c. And I desire that on the death or second marriage of my said Wife my business of Farmer and Market Gardener at Westmarsh in the Parish of Ash next Sandwich shall vest in my Executors and Trustees the aforesaid Edward Lillott and Joseph Lillott my Sons who shall hold the same with the same powers of management as hereinbefore directed as well as the investment and application of the said estate as previously directed in trust for all my children when living shall I hereby direct that when the whole of my children shall have attained the age of twenty one years that then all my real leaseholds and personal estate shall be divided equally among them share and share alike, for their absolute use and benefit And I desire as far as concerns this trust that the vacancies occur from death or otherwise from disclaimer incapacity or departure from England such vacancy be supplied by the Trustee or Trustees remaining and by a majority of my children And I desire that as

well

well as my said Wife that the other Trustees of this my Will shall be chargeable only to the extent of her or his or their respective receipts and shall be exempt from involuntary copies and be entitled to retain all expenses incident to the execution of this my Will And I further declare that should any person or persons interested in this my Will resort to legal proceedings to invalidate the same he or she shall utterly forfeit any part or shares therein of so thereon And I hereby appoint my said wife Jane Lillott Executrix and my sons Edward Lillott and Joseph Lillott Executors and Trustees of this my Will contained in one sheet of four pages In witness whereof I have hereunder set my hand this sixteenth day of December in the year of our Lord One thousand eight hundred and seventy two

Signed by the said Testator as his last Will and Testament in the presences of us present at the same time who at his request in his presence and in the presence of each other have subscribed our names as witnesses

Edward Lillott

George Elgee Turner Gentleman Preston next Wingham
George Levinson Churchman Preston next Wingham

Proved at Canterbury 20th September 1886 by the Oaths of Jane Lillott Widow the Relict and Edward Lillott and Joseph Lillott the Sons the Executors to whom Admon was granted
The Testator was late of Westmarsh in the Parish of Ash near Sandwich in the County of Kent Farmer and died 15th August 1886 at Westmarsh aforesaid

Gross £ Net £1194.17.11   Emmerson & Co Solicitors Sandwich

Aunty Betty and Julie were excited by the news. There would be a lot to fit in when they visited Kent. Mum and Aunty Betty both wrote returning letters to Nan and Doreen. Upon receiving letters from Nan, another family member had been in contact. Cousin June, as Mum and Betty called her, and her husband, Reg. June's father, Frederick Lilliott, was my gran's brother.

The list of people to meet and places to visit seemed to be getting longer by the minute. Mum was so enlightened by all the news coming her way. Nan had sent a black and white postcard of two houses and a bungalow. On the back, Nan had written,

"Many thanks for your letters. I look forward to meeting you sometime. My bungalow is in the centre of the village, on the opposite side of the road on this card. I have a few photos for you to see.
Kind regards, Nan."

At the bottom of the postcard, it read *Scenes of interest and beauty from Preston in Kent.*

Mum replied straight away, letting Nan know the dates of when they would be visiting. Mum desperately wanted to meet Nan with so many questions to ask, too.

With so much news and information, Mum, Betty, and Julie postponed their trip to Kent until May of the following year. It would give them quite a few months to catch up with their family research. Mum and Betty wrote letters asking for more information about the family. Julie started researching on the internet for links connecting to the family ancestry and was growing by the letter.

Mum wrote to Nan explaining they were delaying their visit to next year, as there was so much information being sent to her and her sister, Betty, that they needed to go through the History that was mounting up and needed more research. So everything could be included when they visited Kent and could cover everything. Mum got slightly concerned as she had not heard from Nan until January of the following year.

Dear Joyce,

I am so sorry to be so late in answering your letter, but I have been rather under the weather. I have had eye trouble for one thing, in fact, I lost the sight of my right one suddenly one day, luckily the sight returned after an hour or so. The doctor is treating me for anaemia etc, and I am attending the hospital every so often. This of course has made me to be wary of too much strain on the eyes. Hence my correspondence had to be neglected. You ask in your letter who Winifred, Millicent, Richard, and Ernest, Pam Lilliott were in the Lilliott family well they were the family of Richard (Uncle Dick) who was stepbrother to your grandfather. Winifred, Richard, and Ernest are all dead now. But "Millie" and "Pam". Pam, the youngest is married and Milly who is 88 now lives with them in Canterbury.

My cousin Gwen who was a Griggs (her mother Rose Lilliott) married Ernest Lilliott (second cousin) and on Saturday last Gwen celebrated her 80th birthday and her children gave her a party which was attended by all the cousins etc. Well, Pam and her husband were there. (sister-in-law and well as a cousin) and I gave Pam your letter to read.

Consequently, she is making a call to your cousin Mrs Stockley shortly, Pam will know more about Westmarsh School than I do, for my parents left Sheerwater Farm just before I was five when we went to Preston to live.

She also received letters from the Schoolmaster's son, and you may now get further. Well, I only hope you can fathom this rigmarole out, however, when you pay me a visit I may be able to explain in detail and in a more orderly fashion.

Hoping you are keeping well.

Kind regards, and all best wishes for 1988.

Yours, Nan.

Chapter 6

It was the morning of the journey to Canterbury. Julie would pick up Aunty Betty and Mum at about 9 am; they would visit Canterbury first to see the cathedral and the churches, then make their way to Chislet, Preston, Ash, Westmarsh, Upstreet, and Grove. There would be a lot to fit in over the weekend.

They arranged to meet Nan, Marie, who lived at Sheerwater Farm, and cousin June along the way.

The sun shone, and the roads were clear. Aunty Betty and Mum were thrilled by all the news of their dear Mother's family. At long last, they could put pictures of the faces and places my gran had spoken of as a child growing up on Sheerwater Farm.

Canterbury Cathedral was the first stop and was a lot larger than they thought. The chapel of the Black Prince was also visited, where they thought about Deryk Carver.

Preston was next on their list of visits to meet with Nan Barlow, but she wasn't in. It was surprising as it had been arranged to meet her today. Nan's neighbour came out and explained that Nan had gone to stay at her daughter's for a while, and she hadn't mentioned that the family was visiting. She invited Mum, Betty, and Julie for a 'chat and a cuppa.' They were disappointed Nan wasn't there, but the chat with the neighbour was lovely, and the cup of tea was a much-needed refreshment.

Chislet was next on the agenda. The Norman church of The Virgin St. Mary was a peaceful, beautiful, idyllic country church with wonderful stained-glass windows, an ancient baptismal font, and a quaint organ. As Julie went through the parish records, there it was. The Marriage of her grandparents.

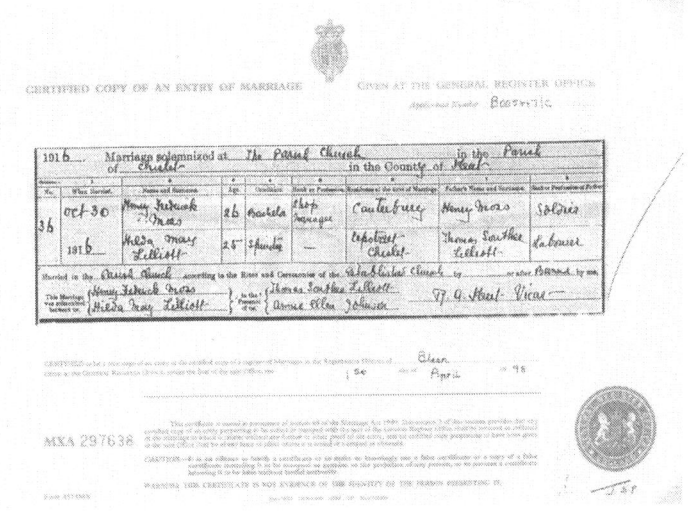

"How wonderful, Julie." Mum filled up with emotion. "Look, Bett, Mother and Father's wedding certificate,"

Julie ordered copies for our family.

Next, they went to visit their cousin June. June's husband Ray opened the door with open arms and smiled.

June, Ray and Betty

They were having a lovely chat with lots of reminiscing. June also thanked Mum for finding their cousin Harry Leaver. She had written to him and received a letter which read he would be flying over from Australia to visit them in late Summer that year with Annie, his brother Frank Lilliott's widow.

June gave her long-lost family a tour around the surrounding hamlets. Frederick, her father, had also been a farmer in Upstreet, Chislet. She showed them the house where her parents had once lived and their Aunt Ruth's village school where she had taught. June enjoyed sharing their history and showing them around wherever they wanted to go.

Frederick's House

The school where Ruth taught

They walked around the cemetery at Ash and saw where their Aunt Annie and grandparents' graves were.

Thomas Southee Lilliott Died in 1917 on May 11th—row 20. No. 18 at Ash. Sarah Ann Castle Died in 1922 on 7th November at the age of 62.

They saw Preston village school, where their Mother had studied, and then journeyed onto Grove, where a lovely pub called The Grove Ferry stood on the bank of the River Stour. The Ferryman had now gone, and a bridge had replaced the chain ferry.

Small boats had moored with people taking trips up and down the scenic river. They decided to have some food and to compare the old photos against the new ones.

"I can't believe that just a hundred years ago," said Mum, "Our family was using this part of the river to transport their produce. Now we, their grandchildren, are sitting here eating food from a pub."

"How times have changed," replied Betty.

The Grove Ferry

The scenery was unchanged.

A lot of photos were taken, and many memories were shared. The scenery hadn't changed In the picture taken across the meadow from Upstreet to Chislet.

Looking across to Upstreet from Chislet.

Yew Tree Cottage

After lunch, June took them to Yew Tree Cottage in Upstreet, where their Mother and family had lived after leaving Sheerwater Farm.

Everyone was exhausted and decided to have an early night. June headed home as the family stayed at a nearby Bed and Breakfast. They would pick her up tomorrow when they would drive to Sheerwater Farm.

The following morning, Julie returned to Ash, where she, Betty, and Mum visited St. Nicholas Church and stayed for the Sunday morning service, remembering Helen Griggs when she had played the church organ there.

They picked up June after the church service, who walked with them for miles around the area and took in the scenery from across the fields. Although the four found it quite exhausting, it was worth every mile.

Lastly, they all wanted to visit Sheerwater Farm, where their Mother and June's father, Frederick, lived as children. As Julie turned the corner in the car, she noticed the sign. SHEERWATER WESTMARSH. They held their breath and awaited in anticipation until the rambling old farmhouse, where their Mother had spoken of love and beautiful days, came into view.

Mum phoned Marie to let her know they were on their way.

Here, they were told, with the warmest memories about Sheerwater Farm, and the farmhouse exceeded their expectations.

Marie and her family showed Mum, Betty, Julie, and June around the once-used diary, with its large, uneven flagstone floor, where their Mother once mentioned she had helped her mum, Sarah Ann Castle, pat the butter into shape before wrapping the yellow creamy spread. Although the building was under refurbishment and had widow replacements, the old inglenook fireplace remained. They could imagine Mother with her family sitting around the raging fire, singing songs and telling their stories about the day across the marshes and surrounding land.

Mum didn't want to leave; she said she could have quite happily stayed and couldn't understand why her Mother and Father had moved away to Portsmouth so soon after they were married, as the area where her Mother had been born was a picturesque haven.

Chapter 7

Mum got home exhausted, happy though, and content with all they had seen and couldn't wait to get the photos from the weekend developed. She was disappointed that Nan hadn't been in and was sure there would be a good reason.

Mum started watching painting programmes on television and started to paint using paint by numbers.

Dad and I helped Mum clear out the spare back bedroom. We had always called the room the back bedroom, which made perfect sense as that was where it was at the back of their three-bedroom house. It was a small room wallpapered in a delicate pink dog rose print. The room was large enough for Mum to set up an easel with paints and brushes. Dad put some shelves up which over time, housed autobiographies written by well-known celebrities.

By the window sat an oversized oyster cane chair, pink in colour. The little room faced south in the afternoons, and it captured the sun.

The view from the window overlooked a field that occasionally homed a few Friesian cows that had belonged to Enborne Gate Farm. The old farmhouse was just in view behind an old Chestnut Tree. In the distance was Combe Hills, Inkpen. On a clear day with binoculars, you could see the outline of Combe Gibbet.

Mum took her typewriter and writings into her room, where her stories and paintings unfolded.

A sign was written in large print next to the chair.

CHANGE IS PROGRESS

Her first attempt to paint freehand was a few poppies onto a rather large white flat plate she had bought from a charity shop. Mum had picked up the idea from Nan's mum when she saw the beautifully painted plate for which Helen Griggs had received an award. With a picture of some poppies to copy from, first, she mixed the green and started to paint the Poppies' stems, but it was more challenging than it looked. The paint just seemed to separate. After hours of trying and not getting anywhere, Mum decided to try painting on canvas instead. When she had finished standing back from her attempt, she was astonished at how good the picture looked.

Dad and I were also impressed and encouraged her to start painting classes to improve her technique. Mum loved to paint the countryside and scenery, but when it came to painting the sky, it just didn't look right, even when she tried covering the canvas in a blue wash and then adding sunsets, sunrises, and clouds. But nothing seemed to work. Mum was at a total loss. I suggested leaving out the sky; nobody would notice as she put so much colour and detail into her pictures. It worked a treat. Mum just didn't paint the skies. Not one person ever commented or asked why.

The West Woods at Marlborough

Spring

Summer

Autumn

Winter

Mum had written a few letters to Nan and was concerned that she'd had no response. She and Betty were also surprised that she hadn't been home the day they arranged to meet. June had written and sent a postcard to Mum and had also written to Betty and Julie.

Mum and Julie were still researching the Huguenots and Lilliott family, and using Newbury Library was a weekly event. Harry Leaver and Annie were true to their word, and although in their seventies, both journeyed from Australia to England to meet their long-lost family and to follow their family tree. Mum, Betty, and Julie spent the day with Harry and Annie, sharing photos and stories. They were only staying in the UK for two weeks, spending most of the time in Kent. They would go with June, who would take the trip with them, starting at Sandwich, where The Lilliotts had first landed from France, and would follow their journey to The Grove Ferry. June would show them around the area, the farmland their forefathers had once owned, and the tales of the family through the ages. Marie had kindly allowed more of the family to look around Sheerwater Farm.

Harry was also a farmer in Australia before he retired; he had never had children or been married. It was the same as Annie and Frank; they had also been farmers but never had children.

Mum and Betty never saw Harry or Annie again, but they kept in correspondence through letters and always sent Christmas cards.

It was the end of the summer when Mum received a letter from Nan.

Dear Joyce,

Many apologies for not informing you that I should be away from home in May. I was so sorry when I returned from my daughter's in Hastings to hear of your lost journey. I went away earlier than I expected, only having four days' notice, and I'm afraid at 86, one is none too bright at times to remember all one's duties.

However, my neighbour has told me she had a very pleasant chat with you and your cousin, and I hope the trip to Preston was not too disappointing after all.

I have not been too well this year, hence the early holiday for a change, but I will be here now to the late autumn (all being well) when I go to Hastings.

I hope you enjoyed your stay in Canterbury. What a miserable summer we are having so far, and the longest day is now gone.

Please excuse my writing. My eyesight is none too good these days.

I am so very sorry to have missed you.

Kind regards,

Nan

Enclosed was a copy of the Poor of the Parish from the 1700s in Westerham of Thomas Lilllot. Mum never heard from Nan again.

[No. 18.]

Kent
To wit. WE whose Names are hereunto subscribed and Seals affixed being the ———

Church Wardens, and Overseers of the Poor of the Parish of *Hendrich* ——— in the *County* of *Kent* aforesaid, do hereby own and acknowledge *Thomas Lillyat, Victualler and Elizabeth his wife now residing in the parish of Westerham in the said County* ——— to be *our* Inhabitants legally settled in the Parish of *Hendrich* aforesaid. IN WITNESS whereof we have hereunto set our Hands and Seals this *First* Day of *August* in the *11* Year of the Reign of our Sovereign Lord *George the Third* by the Grace of God of *Great Britain, France* and *Ireland*, King, Defender of the Faith, and in the Year of our Lord 1771.

Attested by
Willm Donst
James Waters

John Wingate
John Cooper
Geo Wilmott
John Sisley

Churchwardens
Overseers

To the Church-Wardens and Overseers of the Poor of the Parish of *Westerham* ——— in the *said County* ——— of *Kent* ——— or any or either of them

WE whose Names are hereunto subscribed, two of His Majesty's Justices of the Peace for the *County of Kent* ——— aforesaid, do allow of the above-written Certificate. AND WE do also certify, That *William Donst* one of the Witnesses who attested the Execution of the said Certificate, ha*th* made Oath before us, That *he* did see the Church Wardens and Overseers, whose Names and Seals are to the said Certificate subscribed and set, severally sign and seal the said Certificate, and that the Names of the said *William Donst and James Waters*, whose Names are subscribed as Witnesses to the Execution of the said Certificate, are of their own proper Hand Writing. DATED the *2* Day of *June* in the Year of our Lord 1772.

T Warde
J Bodicoate

Sold by J. COLES and SON, Stationers, [No. 21.] in Fleet-Street.

Chapter 8

College took a new turn in the following season. The tutor had given all the students in Mum's class an opportunity to have their writings published and each person was given a list of publishers. Each could choose their own written piece or even write a chosen subject to one of these addresses.

Mum was very interested and thought she would do well at writing children's stories. She spent much time in the back bedroom writing and asking Dad and me to read her work. One was about a child going to the hairdressers for the first time.

Adam Goes To The Hairdressers

My name is Adam, today Mummy took me to the hairdresser's to get my haircut. I sat in a swivel chair, and a lady put a smart red gown around me and tied it at the back. Then mummy came over and told the lady how she wanted her to cut my hair. "The front cut quite short because it always grows so quickly there, a tidy up over the ear and not too short at the back please." She said.

The lady picked up the spray, rather like the one daddy uses in the garden, and tiny squirts of water damped my hair. She told me to bend my head down so she could cut the back, and then I closed my eyes while she cut the front.

I sat very still and only moved my head when she told me to. I could feel all the little bits of hair tickling me on my face and neck. Then she said open your eyes, Adam, all finished. She asked mummy if I could have some gel on my hair in front, and mummy said, "Just a little." Then she flicked up my hair and put some on. She then took the gown off and brushed my neck with a soft brush that tickled. I looked in the mirror, I could now see out. The lady asked me if I would like to see the back. I nodded yes, and she took the oval mirror and showed me.

Mummy said how smart I looked, and now it was her turn to have a haircut.

I sat in the swivel chair and kept whirling around until I was giddy and had to stop. Mummy told me to behave myself and to sit properly, so I sat down in a big deep padded Maison chair with buttons. I was nearly swallowed up by it, it was so soft and large.

Ain't grown-ups are funny people; there's one lady whose head is like a porcupine. She had a cap on her head, and a lady was pulling her hair through it.

Then she put some blue paste on with a paste brush, and it smelt a bit funny, too. Another lady was sitting under a big silver helmet that made a noise; her cheeks were very red, and she was fast asleep. Then there was someone else having some bright green and yellow bendy things put in their hair. She looked as though she had come from another planet.

The door opened, and in came a little boy who was crying because he didn't want his hair cut. I told him it was great fun to sit in those swivel chairs that keep going around, and it is very grown up to have gel on your hair. His mummy asked him if he would like his hair cut like mine; he nodded and stopped crying and went and sat in a chair when the lady called his name.

Mummy looked very smart with her new haircut, and she told me she was very proud of me because of the way I helped the little boy. I thanked the lady for cutting my hair, and mummy said we would see her in six weeks. Do you think the other little boy will also be there? I did find out what his name was. The same as mine, Adam.

Joyce Lilliott Warne.

This was written in pencil in mum's neatest handwriting.

Adam And The Magic Bubble Pipe.

Adam was a little boy who had a bubble pipe. One day in the garden, when blowing bubbles, a giant one appeared. It got bigger and bigger until he found himself floating away inside. Up and away, he went over the rooftops and chimneys with all of the Ariel's reaching out to the sky. Adam soared over the fields that looked like a patchwork quilt. He waved hello to the scarecrow who stood guarding the yellow corn. The world looked like a big place from up there. Adam never imagined there was so much sky, and he had it all to himself. He saw a train wending its way through the green and flowery countryside; the smoke from the engine rose upwards and covered the bubble in a thick grey-like mist. Oh dear said Adam. I hope I don't get lost; it's just like being out in the fog if, by magic, the smoke cleared and the train faded away into the distance. He was now over a busy town, and down below, the people looked rather like insects as they hurried to and fro. Aren't grown-ups funny people thought Adam? Now I know what mummy means when she says she had a busy day.

The bubble was now climbing higher, and puffs of cloud as soft as down drifted by. The clouds reminded Adam of the seeded dandelion clock head and floated like miniature parachutes when he gently blew on them. There was a gentle breeze blowing, and the coastline below him was the silver sea, with seagulls wheeling around and calling to each other. Adam was higher than the birds.

Yachts were bobbing up and down on the sea like corks, and there was a speed boat going so fast that the sea all around it was being churned up into a silver spray. Adam thought he would like one of these fast boats when he grew up. Then he saw a lighthouse which looked like a talk white sandcastle. It must be very exciting to sleep in a lighthouse and to wake up and look out of the window when there are giant waves.

Adam felt the bubble slowing down. The sea mist was hiding everything. Very slowly, he was floating down and then plopping. Just as the bubble burst, he heard his mother say softly, wake up, Adam, your tea is ready. He sat up and rubbed his eyes; as they walked from the garden, Adam told his mother about his exciting trip in the marvellous magic bubble.

The End

By Joyce Lilliott-Warne

The manuscript had many typing errors. Mum said she would pay an illustrator to add drawings to children's stories. Both stories were rejected with a note of "kind return". Mum added another sign in the back bedroom:

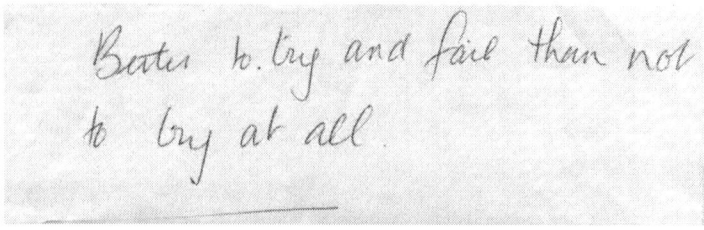

Better to try and fail than not to try at all.

On Sunday afternoons, when the weather was nice, my parents would drive to Kintbury, always popping in to see Mum's sister, Joan, for a cuppa and a catch-up.

Joan thought Mum's paintings and writings were so clever. She was also very wise, which she had inherited from their Mother.
"Your stories are wonderful, Joyce," she said. "But, perhaps writing children's books isn't your forté. Maybe it's to write about what happened to us during WW2?" Mum nodded, smiled, and agreed. "Have you had a walk around The Croft recently? "Joan asked, "And have you had any recollections about Inglewood Cottage? "

From that day, Mum knew what she would write about. Although she had jotted down notes, recorded memories, and written down snippets using the titles from college titles to utilise past experiences. She had never thought about putting everything together into a book. An autobiography.

When they had left Joan's, Dad drove Mum down to The Croft, into Church Lane, and passed someone's home, which years ago had been a shop where Mum had worked when she had first left school. It was called "J. ABRAHAM," She and Dad walked along The Croft and onto the stone pathway past St. Mary's Church.
"Maybe Joan was right," said Mum. "I just had visions of me being a children's author for younger children and having my

books read to them at bedtime." Dad nodded in agreement as he knew Mum wanted that so much.

"Perhaps it's not your story. It may be the market at the moment." Mum shrugged, knowing Dad was showing kindness. They walked through the avenue of blossoms and listened to a very loud blackbird singing its clear, pure song. It was enough to put a smile on Mum's face as she breathed in the clear country air. She would always say she felt calm and at peace in this place and at home. She could think and feel settled.

"Shall we take a walk to Inglewood Cottage?" Dad said, not minding as he enjoyed the stroll.

"That was where we lived as evacuees. It was so cold, the toilet was at the bottom of the garden, we washed in an old copper. We had no running water, just an indoor well where Mother would draw buckets daily to wash, cook, and clean with. At the end of the day, she was too exhausted to draw even for a cup of tea. Poor Mother had such a hard life."

Mum continued reminiscing.

"I still remember Ted when we first left our lovely home in Portsmouth with its mod cons in exchange for Inglewood Cottage, a safe haven with no running water, only a deep inside well in the flagstone scullery. The only heat was from a range. In winter, icy patterns marked the freezing windows. The wind blew through every conceivable opening - but we were safe and could sleep in our beds at night." Dad nodded and took Mum's hand as they walked down the hill towards the three forked roads. Mum continued.

"Us evacuees were welcomed in the village apart from one or two unkind remarks such as 'Portsmouth Slums' and 'Village Interlopers,' which was certainly no fault of our own whichever way you looked at it," She reflected, "But it was a happy ending when we finally settled in."

"Oh look, Joyce," said Dad when they arrived at the cottage. Working in the garden close to the stone wall was a couple who both looked up and smiled. Seeing two smiley faces, Mum told them she had grown up in the house.

"Is the well still there?" She had asked. In unison, they shook their heads. Then the attractive lady said,

"We're told there is a well here somewhere… but nobody knows where. Then she asked. "Do you remember where the well was? If so, could you show us, please?"

Know where the well was? Why! Mum could hardly forget. She led the couple, with Dad following, into the scullery where there was now a thick padded linoleum.

"It's here." She pointed at the place, "It's just here." The couple were delighted and thanked Mum profusely.

On the way home, my parents stopped to visit Mavis, who also lived in the village. Mavis made them both a cup of tea, and the shortbread tin came out. Mum shared with Mavis that she had just shown the couple living at Inglewood Cottage where the well was and that it was covered in thick lino.

"It brought back so many memories, Mave," said Mum.
Reaching into the tin of shortbread, she asked her sister for an honest opinion about what she thought of her paintings and writings.
Mavis agreed with Joan; she loved Mum's paintings and short stories about their younger years and suggested it would be lovely for Mum to start writing and putting her life stories into an autobiography.

When they left Mavis, Mum was feeling a lot brighter. It was ironic that in the following week, someone had written a piece about their war memories in the following weeks, Newbury Weekly News. Dad had phoned Mum at work and had told her about the article, encouraging her to write a piece about her war memories and send it to the Newbury Weekly News. It was printed the following week under the headline **LETTER War-torn memories:**

Reading Mrs Ivy Wells' Mayor's Parlour column last week brought back memories of my own childhood during the Second World War.

I was seven when war broke out and living in Portsmouth with my parents, brother, and sisters. Being one of the main targets for the enemy aircraft. Portsmouth was under constant carriage of heavy, prolonged bombing, and even now, I remember it as a very frightening experience.

We had an Anderson shelter in the back garden, where we had to sleep almost every night. It had four steps down into it and was lined with sandbags. I can almost smell the damp mustiness of it now.

My mother would make flasks of Cocoa and bundles of snacks ready for our "flight into the unknown," as she called it, for we never knew how long we would have to stay in the shelter or if we would ever come out. Several shelters had a direct hit, and you had little chance of survival if this happened.

Our gas masks were always at hand. At the sound of the siren, we would drop everything and head for the safety of the shelter. Once, Mother had made a birthday cake for me and had just put it in the oven when the siren started wailing. We emerged several hours later to find the precious cake burnt to a cinder.

Most nights, the bombardment was deafening, so to try and help deaden the noise, my dad would play the mouth organ, and we would all have a sing-song. This helped to keep our spirits up and made us less afraid.

I remember one day in particular (my sister's and I still talk about it now) when Mother got stuck under the bed during an air-raid. She was rather stout at the time and had crawled there for safety, yelling at us all to do the same. This time, the air raid had taken everyone by surprise, and shrapnel was falling outside. When it was safe to come out from under our beds, we had to lift the bed up from Mother to release her. Her clothing has got caught up in the springs.

After the worst air raid of all Portsmouth, I can remember coming out of the shelter after what seemed an eternity to find the sky bright, debris everywhere, and the acrid smell of smoke hanging in the air. It was at this moment that my parents decided we must leave Portsmouth.

In 1941, my whole family was evacuated to Hungerford. We stayed at The Church House along with many other evacuees. Here we spent a happy six months and had lots of fun.

At last, we did not have to sleep in an air-raid shelter and felt peaceful and safe.

After this, we moved to Kintbury and never went back to Portsmouth. But even now, whenever I hear a siren, it takes me back to my childhood in Portsmouth…

JOYCE LILLIOTT-WARNE
Kingsbridge Road.
Newbury.

Mum had found her confidence again. She started to put her writings together towards her autobiography.

Chapter 9

The new term at college was providing information about poetry. A couple of students in Mum's class had published a few poems and short stories, encouraging her to do the same and turn her hand to poetry.

The Poet's Manual
Traditional Forms in Poetry

The Villanelle

The Villanelle was originally a round song sung by farm labourers; the name comes from the Latin villa or farm. The medieval French villanelles were irregular, but in the sixteenth century, the form became fixed as we know it today.

It is written in tercets rhymed a-b-a until the last stanza. The first stanza furnishes the two refrains, A1-b-A2, and the succeeding stanzas repeat these two lines alternately in the third line of the tercet as the refrain a-b-A1, a-b-A2, etc. Each refrain line must be repeated the same number of times. Then, in the last stanza, a quatrain, they are repeated together, a-b-A1-A2. The poem is frequently composed of five tercets and a closing quatrain but may have three, five, seven, nine, or any odd number of tercets, as desired.

The popularity of the Villanelle has revived somewhat among modern poets, perhaps because it lends itself very well to the creation of the mood. It has been used with memorable success.

Theme With Variation

The article with variations has numerous poetic possibilities. The theme may be original, as it is the first quatrain of the rondeau redouble, or it may be a well-known passage used line by line to set off a chain reaction in the successive stanzas of a new poem. If the theme is original rather than borrowed, it is usually developed seriously, though this is not an invariable rule. If the article is borrowed, it is frequently developed in a surprising, odd, or humorous way.

For that week's homework, the word was Swallows. With Mum's confidence breaking through, she wrote this poem.

SWALLOWS

The swallows are ready to depart,
They will be missed by the throng,
I saw them gathering in the park.

Resting before their journey starts,
Perched on a wire loose and long,
The swallows are ready to depart.

Nests in the eaves are empty and stark,
Fledglings grew quickly and strong,
I saw them gathering in the park.

There is sadness in my heart,
Another summer has gone,
The swallows are ready to depart.

The winter will be cold and dark,
But they'll return on April's song,
I saw them gathering in the park.

In the spring I watched them dip and dart,
Now the thermals will carry them along,
The swallows are ready to depart,
I saw them gathering in the park.

By Joyce Warne

The tutor collected and marked everyone's poetry for the week and said to Mum hers was good enough to publish. Mum was thrilled. The tutor also mentioned that poems were needed for a book called *Poetry*

Now. SOUTH 1992. Mum's poem stood a chance. Mum never said a word to anyone but submitted *Swallows* anyway.

She was over the moon - and so was everyone else - when eventually *Swallows* was published in *Poetry Now*. It was printed on page six. Mum gave me her edition. Inside, she had written *For Sarah with Love from Mum*.

Then, she ordered another ten books. Everyone was so happy for her. Friends and family said, "There is no going back now, Joyce!"

On the back page, it read *This book is one you will want to keep to share with others and go back to on your own -like relaxing with an old friend*.

Mum's work had been officially published in a book, with the ISBN 1 85731 111 6. Spurred on by her success, wrote the following poem:

Stars

The stars were missing from the skies
On those terrible war-torn nights
All I could see were clouds of fire
As the stars were hid from sight

They must be hiding somewhere
In a beautiful heavenly hue
But here while PORTSMOUTH'S burning
There wasn't a star on view

But one day I will find them
Dazzling the skies above
Lit with a special brilliance
From the marvellous hand of GOD,

By Joyce Lilliott-Warne.

Mum's tutor said it was brilliant and to look for a publisher and gave her a leaflet from Anchor Books, which said: *If you like reading and writing poetry, drop us a line or a call, and we'll send you a free information pack.* Mum wrote to them and the package soon arrived. Anchor Books was looking to publish poetry in a book called "Poets for Peace." The attached letter explained: *Anchor Books is a small press established in 1992 to promote readable poetry to an audience as broadly as possible. We want to develop an outlet for writers and poets who may have struggled to see their work in print.*
Mum filled in the form and sent her poem *Stars*. Then she awaited with bated breath. Sending her work address, because as the receptionist it would arrive to her first. She didn't tell anyone and didn't want anyone to be as disappointed as she would be if the poem wasn't published. It read very well. Mum enjoyed writing about memories from her childhood, but it was down to the editor if the poem would be published or not. She waited for over a year for a reply. In the meantime, she just carried on with her writing.

The letter arrived and was headed *Anchor Books*, informing Mum that her poem had been selected for publication in the coming book. Mum couldn't stop smiling. She was still writing her about her family's life in Portsmouth during World War 2 until they had been rehomed to Queens Way in Kintbury, West Berkshire. She would send her manuscript to Anchor Books once finished.

The editor had also written. *The poetry in this book had been selected from many entries. Editing proved to be a difficult and daunting task as the Editor had to make the final selection. The poems chosen represent a cross-section of styles and content. They have been sent from all over the world, written by young and old alike, united in a passion for writing poetry. This selection will delight and please the authors and all those who enjoy reading poetry.*

Poets In Peace was published. *Stars* was on page 84. Mum ordered fifteen copies to be given to friends and family. The back cover blurb read as follows:

Poets for Peace

It is a request to all the governing bodies around the world. A plea to stop all bloodshed and unnecessary sacrifices of innocent victims of war, and a hope that one day, the fighting will finally end.

All the poets included in this enjoyable anthology bring together their deepest emotions on the traumatic events of the war, from the innocent cries of families who have lost someone very close to their hearts to memories of devoted soldiers who survived and remembered the emotional torture suffered during the war.

I'm sure 'Poets for Peace' will bring back a lot of memories and feelings to all readers, which just goes to show how wars throughout the world stick in our minds for life, and we live in the hope that one day we finally see a breakthrough and live with one another in peace and harmony.

A few years later, in 1998, Mavis was doing a lot of voluntary work in Kintbury and was helping quite a bit in St. Mary's Church; she cleaned the brass and arranged the flowers. Often, she would pick up Kintbury villagers from their homes and take them to a coffee morning or other activities around the village. It had been mentioned to Mavis at one of the volunteer meetings that a book about Kintbury would be put together, covering over a century from 1900-1999. The volunteers would put it together from stories written by the Kintbury people. Mavis phoned Mum and told her about it straight away.

Mum had started to assemble her autobiography, and it was almost finished. She had never written anything so significant since her decline about the children's bedtime stories, and she wasn't sure, but she said she didn't have anything to lose, and her writing and typing had improved immensely. She wrote to the Kintbury Volunteers. The piece was called *Inglewood Cottage* by Joyce Warne (nee Moss).

I was nine when I came to Kintbury in 1941. We - that is - Mum and Dad, three sisters (two older, one younger), and an older brother, were evacuees from Portsmouth. We lived at Inglewood Cottage, which was a lovely old house on the edge of the village at the bottom of the hill where three roads meet. Inglewood Cottage, the very name spells enchantment, was a wonderful place to live, for we had a huge garden for play and an apple tree to climb. Distant cornfields glistened under a hot summer sun in the skies. Which seemed endlessly blue. My sisters and I swam in the local canal, then free of narrow boats and polluted water, played cricket and rounders in the High Street with no fear of traffic, and played hide-and-seek amongst the corn stooks. Best of all, in spring, were the picnics in the bluebell woods, eating strawberry jam sandwiches, and drinking lemonade made with a bright yellow powder that fizzed when water was added. Oh! The days of yesteryear. Where have they all gone?

Kintbury was bliss after the bombs of Pompey, where we spent most nights crouching in our Anderson shelter and some days also, as there were fearful air raids with much devastation.

Soon after our arrival at Inglewood Cottage, the vicar of St. Mary's called to see us. Then what a surprise! For it was the very same Rev. Guthrie Allison who had christened my sister Betty before at St.Mary's Church, Portsmouth. What a coincidence, same person, same name of church!

The solitary cottage was deliciously cool in the summertime but an ice box in the winter. Sometimes it was days before the frosted patterns on the sash-type windows went away, after which howling, bitter cold winds found their way down the chimney, through the keyholes and every opening there was and of which there were plenty. On raw wet days, we used to huddle around the black range getting toasted on one side only while our backs shivered. Our water came from an indoor well in the flagstoned scullery. A bucket of water went nowhere for our family of seven, so one heard the constant clanging of the chain which hauled the swaying bucket to the surface, splashing everything in its path, including Mother's sensible shoes and thick stockings. A huge, thick wooden protective cover then dropped back over the deep well with a third that echoed all over the house. To this day, I can still hear that dull, heavy sound. In the corner of the pokey kitchen was a huge stone copper with a fireplace underneath. On wash days the steam would rise in great clouds while Mother pummelled away at the cotton sheets and pillowcases, towels, etc, with an enormous copper stick and a bar of Sunlight soap. Soap powders of the day were Rinso, Persil, and Oxydol.

Milk and Watercress

Near Inglewood Cottage were the watercress beds where for sixpence (21/2p), you could buy a giant bunch of fresh cress to take home for tea. The salad cress was bunched together with a piece of orangey string finished with a loop for carrying. Eaten with crusty Hovis from Mr. Bowsher's bread shop, never did watercress taste so good. Up the hill from the cottage was Sycamore Farm, where again for sixpence, we could get a large jug of creamy milk straight from the cow. When it was my turn to fetch the milk, I could never resist taking a small sip from the enamel jug while walking back down the hill to home.

School

Our younger ones went to St.Mary's School (the old building), while the two older ones went to work in the 'Feathery Flake flour mill down by Kintbury Station. In those far-off days, great trucks would deliver the fine flour to shops and businesses all over Southern England. I was nervous about school because of my stammer, which was truly dreadful. Perhaps the bombing raids of Portsmouth caused it, or it could have been the mastoid operation at the age of seven, which left me with a semi-deaf ear. Or had it been something to do with my being born with six fingers on my right hand? Whatever the cause of my terrible stutter. I was determined to conquer it, and conquer it I did, even though it took years. At school, I found only kindness and understanding and settled in well, making many friends with whom I am still in contact.

Our teachers were kind but very strict and were sticklers for the three R's. One teacher in particular had the biggest false teeth I had ever seen, which clicked like castanets every time she spoke, but I would add here I mean no disrespect to that learned lady. On the contrary, she was an excellent teacher who was loved by all. Another teacher was rather poorly to put it and was rather fond of sitting upon the corner of one's desk, that is until she forgot the inkwells had just that morning been replenished. After that, her ample figure sat at her own desk and in her own chair and was very wary of those tiny pots of ink which caused much hilarity in the classroom. There were no school dinners in those days so we were fortunate enough to live within walking distance of going home to a hot dinner every day. Rabbit was often on the menu with lots of fresh vegetables from the garden, followed by a yummy pudding, such as treacle, jam, or sultana with custard. All washed down with clear, cold well water. This would sustain any hungry being such as me.In those halcyon school days, everyone had free school milk and this was delivered daily in third-pint bottles. When the ground was covered in frost and ice corks topped the tiny bottles, they were to be found thawing out around the coke-burning black tortoise stove in the classroom.

School started with a hymn and finished with prayers. Empire Day on May 24th was honoured yearly. The whole school paraded around the Union Jack which was hoisted in the playground. Cookery classes were held at Hungerford. We had to walk over the bridges to catch a bus at Kintbury crossroads on the A4. I did not enjoy cooking very much but once I did excel at bread-making *and my perfect loaf was on display for all to see. I loved the nature walks to Winterly Woods or the Avenue where there was a place to paddle or sit called 'Granny's Doorstep. 'Does anyone remember this nostalgic place where friends and I spent many happy hours during the golden school summer holidays?*

The Shop

I left school at 14 and worked for Mrs. J. Abraham in the grocery and provision trade. Our shop was at the end of Church Street next to The Croft. I believe the building is now called Church House and is the home of a famous writer and his equally famous dog. Back in 1946, there were five such food shops, two butchers, a newsagent, an outfitter's, a barber's (where I had my hair mop-shaped), several sweet shops, an ironmonger's, and coal yard and Mrs Willoughby's vegetable and fish shop where on Fridays one could get the tastiest fish and chips.

 In Mrs Abraham's shop, the work was interesting but quite hard as nearly everything had to be weighed, including sugar, biscuits, rice, dried fruits, oatmeal and soda, and other goods too numerous to mention. Butter, lard, and sometimes margarine came in blocks of 28lbs. Because there was no fridge or freezer, perishable goods such as fats, cheese, and bacon had to be carried down to the cellar at the close of business and then lugged up the steps in the morning. Phew! Who would do this work now? There were two shop assistants (I was one) and Mrs. Abraham made three. Now and then a part-timer would come in to help out. We had to skin whole cheeses and slice the bacon on a razor-sharp bacon slicer. I remember the part-timer cutting her finger on this slicing machine, causing one customer to faint in a dead heap on our tiled floor at the sight of blood. Only the boss (Mrs Abraham) was allowed to clean the 'rasher machine' as I called it, for its scythe-like slicer was lethal. The lovely old shop as I recall smelt of polish, candles, carbolic soap, mint humbugs, cheese, and above this, the Devon Violets scent worn by my boss.

 What wonderful tasting biscuits we served up in those days. Here are a few of the favourites we sold-Huntley & Palmers Cornish Wafers, Ginger Nuts, Breakfast Rusks and Milk and Honey, Carr's Table Water, Jacobs Custard Creams, which melted in your mouth, Peek Frean's Shortcake, and a very special digestive called Granola made by Mcfarlane Lang. The shop had a doorbell over the top of the door which sounded every time a customer entered. Our motto was 'Service with a smile' and everyone was greeted with a 'Good Afternoon', whichever applied. Thursday was a half-day closing.

Rationing

Rationing was on and the allowance for each person per week was:

8oz. Sugar   2oz. Lard
4oz. Margarine   3oz. cheese
2oz. Butter   4oz. Bacon

Plus one egg and 4. oz. of tea. One dear lady said. "I eat my meagre piece of cheese all in one go as it is better to have one good feed than slice it so thin you can't it".
Another poor soul walked all of two miles back to the shop on a boiling hot day to return her egg, which was bad, in a cup. Dressed in black to her ankles and wearing a wide-brimmed straw hat this lovely lady said with such sweetness" I was so looking forward to my weekly egg for tea". She was not disappointed. After a rest in one of the chairs down by the counter, plus a glass of water to refresh her, she went home with two new-laid eggs from Mrs Abraham's own hens.

Because of food shortages, my mother's sister in Australia sent us goodie parcels containing lard, honey, jam, bacon, fruit, and luncheon meats. These items were most welcome. They helped to stretch our measly rations. Looking back now I often wondered how we all managed on such sparse rations. But we did and people were cheerful as well as good-natured and humble. At least those were who came into the shop. I swept and dusted, filled shelves weighed up, delivered baskets of shopping on foot, fetched and carried from the cellar. All for the princely sum of 12 shillings(60p)per week. My weekly wage. Oh! I almost forgot to mention the sweet ration, which was 4oz. per week. This was torture for most children, including me, so when my friends and I had used our sweet coupons up we bought Rennies indigestion tablets to eat, as they were the nearest things to mints. Can you imagine it? These we chewed while idling away time along the river in glorious weather.

The Coronation Hall and the British Legion Hut.

There was no television in our early lives so most evenings were spent listening to the radio. Favourite programmes were ITMA ("It's That Man Again!"). Dick Barton Special Agent and the Paul Temple series. Once a month there was a dance at the British Legion hut, which was near the Coronation Hall. These dances were highly popular with with people coming in from miles away to a very fine evening of dancing. I remember two outstanding bands which performed there, one was called" The Barn Owls" and the other 'The Gold Stars." Dances of the day were the valeta, quickstep, foxtrot, samba, rumba, and if one was skilled enough the tango, to name but a few. The Corn Exchange Hall also held its fair share of dances, including Olde Tyme dancing, which was well attended not only by the dancers themselves but also by people who sat and watched and listened to the music. Concerts were also held with lots of local talent taking part, including my younger sister, Mavis, who had a lovely singing voice.

The VJ party, celebrating the end of the Second World War, was held in the Coronation Hall. Bunting was strung across the hall and underneath sandwiches, cakes, and jellies were laid out on on long trestle tables. Mother helped make the large bowls of jelly I can see them now as she put them to set on a marble slab in the larder.

We also had a 'Girls Club' back in the early fifties. This was held in the Parish Room on a Monday evening. From an old piano in the corner of the room, one girl rattled out musical tunes for sing-a-long and one of our favourite song songs was 'Deep In The Heart of Texas.'

We gathered in the Parish Room for talks and discussions on whatever was topical. There were about 20 or so of us to plan the coming events, such as dances, plays, fencing matches, quizzes, and card games. We had a marvellous compere for our dances by the name of Mr. B. Harrison of Hungerford.

Autumn

Autumn was my favourite time when I lived in Kintbury. Perhaps it was something to do with the magnificent copper beeches surrounding Inglewood Cottage, for it was then that the trees took on the most glorious hues of red, amber, and orange. The colours were a joy to behold. Followed by yet more joy as the tall beeches discarded their tired leaves for me to shuffle through.

Another reason why I loved the autumn was the Harvest Festival in the little chapel. I can visualise now the pyramid of fruits and the variety of vegetables on display. Smell the earthy goodness of the sheaves of corn in the packed chapel as we stood to sing' We Plough the fields and scatter'. Our contribution to this fine produce was from our Blenheim apple tree, which yearly yielded a massive crop of scrumptious eating apples. Inside Inglewood Cottage bowls of eating apples permeated the house. Outside in a cardboard box were windfalls for people to help themselves.

The evening following Harvest Festival, all of the delicious goods, i.e. jams, jellies, pickles, beans, tomatoes, beetroots, onions, potatoes, and, breads were *auctioned off in the chapel. Buttoned up against the chill night air my sister and I, along with Mother, would go to this sale of produce where for just a few pence one could fill a very large bag full of fruit and vegetables. To this day my sisters and I still talk about Mrs. Willoughby's Harvest Festival.*

A Step from Kintbury

I lived in the village until the fifties, when I got married in St Mary's Church and moved to Newbury. However, I am still in contact with the village because my family settled there and I am only a step from Kintbury myself.

Mum sent the copy to Kintbury Volunteer Group and soon had a reply letter saying her piece was gratefully received and would be printed in their book *Kintbury-A Century Remembered 1900-1999*. Mum simply couldn't believe it; her two sisters were right. This was her forté.

Chapter 10

The last few publications had given Mum a powerful mindset. She worked hard writing her autobiography, called *That Summer*. The name had come about when she had been a child, there had been a sequence of mishaps throughout the summer months where everything had gone wrong. My gran would always talk about it.

"Do you remember *That Summer*?" she would say.

Once the manuscript had been thoroughly read, checked, and neatly typed, with Mum's sisters and my dad reading it and giving positive feedback, Mum sent the hopeful book to the publishers in Peterborough.

She was thrilled she had worked on finally getting a book published for so many years. The book *That Summer* would bring hope and inspiration to so many readers. It had been written with inspiration, sharing love, fun, and everyday hardship.

But the manuscript had been returned and rejected, with a cover letter explaining the work wasn't really what they would be looking to publish, but thank you. Mum was very quietly upset. The manuscript was placed into a blue folder and left on the side, in the lounge amongst her reading books and forgotten about. Mum decided college and writing wasn't for her anymore. The typewriters were now a distant memory and given to a charity shop, but she did decide to carry on with her paintings.

Two years later, on September 26th, 2004, my dear Mummy Joyce passed away. She was seventy-one years old and had been living with a terminal illness for the last ten years, never grumbling or moaning about her health. If you had met her, you would never have realised how Ill she was.

Mum's ashes were buried in her favourite place in St Mary's church grounds by The Croft, Kintbury, West Berkshire.

Joyce Warne (nee Moss)
January 15th 1932 – September 26th 2004

Part Two
Introduction

After Mum had passed away, life wasn't the same. There was a void. I'm guessing it was how she had felt after losing her own Mother. Dad had asked me to read Mum's manuscript, which was still in the same place where she had placed it. But I couldn't. My life had been full of fun with picnics, jelly, and ice cream, so idyllic it could have been out of a storybook; I felt if I had read Mum's autobiography, it would have changed my perception. Dad had asked me to move in with him, which I did gladly.

In the back bedroom, Mum's little haven, Dad had put her belongings of stories and artwork into a box. Although I was an only child, I had been offered all of Mum's drawings and writings. I couldn't face reading or going through anything. I just wanted my memories to stay unchanged.

The box was full of Mum's projects. Her paints, which Dad had so lovingly wrapped, were placed on top. Adam, my son, who loved to draw and paint, welcomed the gift. Something inside had left me when she had taken her last breath. Life would never be the same. Dad would often point over to the blue folder and say,

"I guess you will read your mum's manuscript in your own time."

I would just nod, with no intention. A few years later, Dad passed away, too. His ashes are buried with Mum's. Kintbury would always remain a big part of my life.

Chapter 1

With Dad's departure, my life changed radically. I had decided to put all my spare time into decorating their house. It was strange not to hear my parents laughing or Mum chatting on the phone. Mum's oyster chair was still in the back bedroom. The delicate wallpaper print that she had chosen brought back loving memories. I sat on the pink oyster chair, looking out of the window. The gibbet was still in view, but the field that once the Friesian cows roamed and chewed their cud, was now; houses and a road were now my direct view. I decided to leave this room as it was.

I would start decorating the main bedroom first, although my bed was in there, as Dad had slept downstairs when I had moved in. Only the walls to be painted here in a soft white and with the aid of my friend Bev, an interior designer, who helped and made the most beautiful flowing blackout curtains with a pleated headed pelmet to finish, a pale lemon with large bold Lilly print, they certainly gave the bedroom a warm but modern look.

The lounge would be the next room to freshen up; the hospital bed was now gone. The corner sofa with soft furnishings had just finished the space and complimented the Fleur de Lys curtains and Heritage Georgian painted walls. Mum's reading books were placed back onto the shelves and into the exact place they had been before decorating. Mum's blue folder was also replaced where she had left it. The thought hadn't even entered my mind to open the folder, let alone to read it.

The dining area would be next on the list. The walls were painted in a lime whitewash with long Laura Ashley curtains. I added grandeur by having a large chandelier installed. With the open fire still in use, I recalled the Christmas family get-togethers.

Mum with her centrepiece made from an idea from the television show Houseparty.

The smell of dad's mulled wine wafted from the kitchen on a Christmas day morning, singing and dancing to Frank Sinatra, Dean Martin, and Sammy Davis Junior, The Rat Pack, as they were called.

"Good Ol' Frankie." Mum would say.

Cards and Monopoly would be ready for when the family arrived. I looked at Mum's table. The scratch made by the heavy electric typewriter was still showing in the grain, and I ran my fingers over it. Mum was so happy when her poems and her Kintbury piece were published. I pushed her rejected works and the manuscript to the back of my mind; I wasn't even ready to think about that. It had come to mind that I would never read *That Summer*.

Dad's sideboard containing his drinking glasses were all different shapes depending on the liquor it held; the other side of the cabinet still encased was his VSOP, cherry brandy, Glenfiddich, and a few bottles of baby chams. These would never be opened or drunk. I would hold the memories close. The Harveys Bristol Cream stood alone, making me smile, thinking of Mum as she would say,

"We don't have sherry in our house. We serve Harveys."

The flooring of the home would be the last thing to replace. Dad had left money to be put into place to modernise, and we had discussed decor and colour. Our tastes were similar, now having to update the kitchen with mod cons, although it would be expensive, it would prove cost-effective.

Dad and I had always wanted an American fridge freezer, as Dad and I had called it when visiting Dorothy in Florida and seeing hers. When it arrived, it was as big as my double wardrobe, with its stainless steel finish, water tap, and two ice cube shapes, one for crushed ice, the other function formed half crescents looking like tangerine segments.

The kitchen would be designed around this state-of-the-art food storage. I kept the red quarry tiles, "Such a pain to keep clean," I would hear Mum say.

The split-level cooker matched the stainless-steel finish of the fridge freezer, and the Neff top oven hob fitted snugly in the alcove. I kept the kitchen wall tiles, knowing how much Mum loved the plainness of each with a hand-painted motif of cherries. A heavy door curtain with matching curtains with a plain background with a large bold print of random cherries and foliage matched the wall tiles. With white kitchen units, it just finished off the look—only the bathroom to tackle. The hall would be decorated last with its high ceilings and carpeting.

The bathroom was a challenge. My parents' bath was tucked under the window and ran along the wall length. The shower was a separate cubicle at the side of the bath with the sink and toilet adjacent. Mum had loved it at first with its blue and pink flower transfer pattern and the gold taps, but over time, the transfer had peeled away, the gold taps had tarnished, and it was time for a definite change.

The p-shaped bath I had spotted would fit perfectly along the other side of the wall, which meant the sink placement would have to be changed, and the toilet would have to be moved across by an extra three inches. I realised the amount of work and additional pipes needed. When the black slate tiles had been laid on the bathroom floor, and the travertine wall tiles had been tiled up to the ceiling, it looked even better than I had expected.

After a week or two, when the bathroom was ready, I asked the plumber to return to add a power shower. The rose head went up to the ceiling at the widest p-shaped part of the bath. Hair washing would be a lot easier, too, with a separate hand-held shower head attached to the side.

The house felt like living in a 5-star hotel. It was modern, practical, and easy to run, with the white lime wash being painted from the dining room throughout to the hall and landing and with a pale cream carpet running into every room, apart from the bathroom and kitchen. The house was complete. It just needed new towels for the finishing touch.

Although I lost both parents very close together and only being thirty-nine years old when Mum died, the project on the house was an outstanding achievement. I felt I would have made my parents proud. I sat in the kitchen, sipping tea and looking out from the large window into the south-facing garden. Mum's favourite blossom was out on the syringa tree, the tiny white flowers smelling of orange blossom intertwined with the scented dog rose. The garden would be one area that I would never change.

Chapter 2

I remember the day well. It was a scorching May bank holiday. I had decided to meet with some school friends in Newbury Town Centre for coffee and a catch-up. I had finished shopping in the Laura Ashley sale, buying soft Egyptian cotton towels, and was looking forward to putting them into the now-finished bathroom. The decorating had been a massive challenge; now it was all finished, I would invite friends for dinner parties and soirées.

Making my way towards the coffee shop with my towel bales, feeling the warmth of the May sunshine on my face, I smiled a proper feel-good smile. It was my first smile for the first time since losing my parents. My friends were already sitting on the silver cafe chairs with matching tables, sipping their cappuccinos in the Marketplace, waving as I walked toward them.

We ordered brunch and caught up with our news, and they decided to come to mine on the coming Friday evening; we would get a takeaway and watch a film. We departed after a few hours, and instead of going straight home, I drove over to Kintbury and visited Mum and Dad's place of rest. I popped in by chance to see Aunty Mavis, but she wasn't in, so I journeyed back to Kingsbridge Road.

Parking up and walking up to the front door, I put my key into the lock, but as soon as I opened the door, I knew something was seriously wrong.

I'm not sure if it was the noise I had heard first, but as I entered the hallway, the beautifully painted walls were streaming down the walls along with plaster! My feet were standing in an inch of water! The ceiling was bowing where water had accumulated, and it looked like an elephant was sitting on it from upstairs. Water was spewing out through the chandelier. I ran upstairs, but even in that short time, I had become drenched from the downpour of water. I knew I had to act fast. Water was pouring from every ceiling, down the walls. The noise was deafening. It was as if I was in a

thunderous waterfall. In these situations, if someone had asked me.
"What would you save in a situation like this?"
I would have answered.
"My clothes".
In reality, I knew I would lose everything very soon from the ferocity of the water, and my clothes could be replaced. I had to get help and fast. The source of the water had to be stopped.

As I ran down the stairs, I grabbed my Grandad's First World War medals, which hung on the wall, in a picture frame that Dad had so carefully positioned, was now sodden.
"My father was so brave," Dad had said. "Fighting at Ypres, in the trenches, he was also in the Battle of the Somme and had received The Mons Star."
I'm not sure what he would have thought about me. In this situation, I wasn't feeling at all brave. I grabbed Dad's blue suede Marks and Spencer moccasin slippers, which I'd kept at the bottom of the stairs. Keeping them had made it feel like he was close by.
As I got to the front door, I had to get help. The living room door was wide open, and Mum's blue folder caught my eye. I grabbed it, not because I wanted it, but because I knew that at that moment it would be the only thing I would have left of my Mum's. I remember going out of the front door with these three items in my hand, screaming, knowing I had lost everything.

The neighbours had come out of their houses when they heard my cries for help. I was drenched from head to toe and in a state of shock. I phoned the plumber, who was at a barbecue out of town. He came as quickly as he could, but by the time he arrived, two ceilings had come down from the sheer weight of the water. The culprit of the flood was that the T-bar that had attached the two water tanks had come apart from the main water supply coming into the attic, with no stopper; the water was gushing out from the mains water supply straight into the house. The insurance company could only come out to look at the property until three days after the event, and I couldn't touch anything for insurance purposes. I couldn't even go into the house; the electricity had blown, everything was soggy and ruined from water damage. At that moment, I knew how Mum had felt when she and her family had to evacuate their home in Portsmouth with her one doll and my grandma with her one dress.

The ceilings were all checked for asbestos; they were all clear. Piece by piece, my parents' furniture was removed from the family home, along with all my surrounding memories and securities to all be thrown into a skip. I couldn't look at the dining table with the typewriter scratch, along with Mum's oyster chair that she so dearly loved to sit in.
"It's my thinking chair," she would say with her heartwarming smile.
The carpets were pulled up, and the cream colour and thick pile were gone. Now, it was nothing but a soggy-smelling, dirt-looking rag. Massive electric fans and condensers were put into the house to absorb the moisture, and it would take nine months to dry. I was told that if I hadn't have returned in time, I wouldn't have had a place to return to.

Friends rallied around with everything one would need for a bottom drawer. After the nine months were up and the home was dry, the plasterers turned up, and after another five months, the building started to look like a house of dwelling- but I could still smell the damp, and it had a harmful effect on my asthma.

The contents insurance paid out a hefty cheque to a shop of choice, a pine shop replacing old with new. I just wanted my parents' furniture back. Life just wasn't and wouldn't ever be the same again. Gran had said everything happens for a reason, but I honestly couldn't see why.
After looking around the pine showroom and putting the order together, I handed the big cheque to the over-smiley man in the shop, who said it would take about ten weeks for the furniture to be delivered.
"It's all handmade, and the drawers have dovetail joints; all the furniture should be with you Christmas week."

Two weeks before Christmas, I received a letter in the post from an official receiver; the furniture shop, who had taken my cheque and cashed it, had gone into bankruptcy. The cheque I received with the letter was for £1.52. The insurance company wouldn't pay out again.

Dorothy, Mum's friend, had flown from Florida and stayed at The Hilton for Christmas. She had invited me to join her. It was just the lift I needed, and I was also feeling down as I was still receiving Christmas cards from Harry in Australia and Mum's cousins June and Reg. But this year and for always, I could never return any correspondence as I had lost their addresses and everyone's phone numbers in the flood. All the hard work Mum had done to trace down the Lilliot family had all now gone!

Dorothy cheered me up immensely, and after having a wonderful Christmas with her and feeling clear-headed, I decided to move out of Kingsbridge Road and start again, taking cuttings from the dog rose, syringa, lavender plant, and Dad's rosemary bush, which he would add to lamb on the Sunday roast and new potatoes. As I locked the door for the last time, holding my garden cuttings, Mum's unopened blue folder, and Dad's moccasins, I knew I would never come down this road again. The memories were far too painful.

Chapter 3

The years had flown by. The one-bedroom cottage was perfect. It was warm and cosy with a south-facing garden. The first thing I did when I moved in was to plant the tenderly loved cuttings. I placed Dad's slippers at the bottom of the stairs and put Mum's blue folder on the bookshelf in the alcove opposite the soft grey sofa.

I painted the cottage with help from friends using a colour called Strong White by Farrow and Ball. It lightened the place. Bev had made curtains and fixed all the blinds. The carpets in the house were the same colour as the new ones I'd laid in Kingsbridge Road. The previous tenant had left all the white kitchen goods.

I wasn't repurchasing new, and quite honestly, I couldn't afford it. I bought furniture from a second-hand project shop on the Bone Lane Estate in Newbury with a new neighbour and friend, Marcy, who helped me sand and repaint the furniture with white B&Q paint.

The cottage began to take shape; I was starting to feel at home. I had reframed Grandad's war medals and passed them on to Adam, who proudly placed them on the wall.

Over the next few years, I accumulated many items in The Cottage, which my friends called my home "The Doll House"- very apt for the quaintness. But it had started to feel cluttered. With a large basket, I sifted through the items that had no use. I filled a basket, along with Dad's slippers. Mum's blue folder came into sight. I would never open the blue folder, so I placed it on top of the pile and went to the recycling dustbins.

Marcy was doing a spot of weeding and stopped to chat, asking me what I was throwing out as she would like the basket if that was going out for rubbish, too. She had also asked what was in the blue folder. I replied that my Mum had written her memoirs entitled *That Summer*. I would never read it as I may be upset about what I read. Marcy had answered nicely that it wasn't mine to throw away and that maybe my children or grandchildren would like to read it one day. She was right. It wouldn't be right to throw it away. It was placed back onto the shelf, even though it always caught my eye. It would just be left there.

I was fifty-four years old when the pandemic broke out. I had been feeling quite rough for the last few days and took a COVID test. I had tested positive! It was the second time I'd had Covid. The first time I contracted this virus, I was so scared I thought I might die and phoned the emergency number for advice. My oxygen levels had dropped to 92, satisfactory as long as they weren't under 90. It was okay; feeling so breathless, I upped my asthma inhaler, drank lots of water and paracetamol, and crawled into bed. It was a lot like the flu with aches, pains, and high temperature, but this virus also gave you a headache and a cough. Many people struggled to breathe, and sometimes, it felt like one's lungs were being squeezed. I had laid in bed with no energy for a good two weeks; although I was feeling better, one could still transfer the virus if you still tested positive. Some people were testing positive with no symptoms.

The second time I contracted COVID, I hadn't been near anyone at all, but I just knew I had got it. The peppery taste in my mouth and my taste buds were no more. The headache was terrible this time, with flushed cheeks and a raging high temperature. Having no energy to climb the stairs, I made a bed on the sofa, took paracetamol every four hours, and drank plenty of fluids.

I did manage to open the window for some fresh air, and as I lay on the sofa, the brilliant warm sunshine pouring in, I must have dozed off.

I'm not sure what time I awoke. Still, the position of the sunshine streaming through the cottage window was bouncing off my mirrored tissue box, which made a prism of an arched rainbow straight onto Mum's blue folder, whether it was COVID, too many paracetamols, or something else. Still, that folder looked bright and pulled me towards it.

As I picked up the faded blue folder and opened it, the frail paperwork, half typed and half written in Mum's finest handwriting of twenty years ago, was ready to be read. As I took out the manuscript, The front page read *That Summer by Jussie. E Lilliot.*

I turned over the next page when Mum's four-season paintings fell out. The beautiful colours hadn't faded over time. Even if they were faded, I would still have been framing them. I read *That Summer* through, I laughed and cried; in fact, I wept. I re-read the wonderfully inspiring autobiography again. The story was beautiful. It felt like Mum was reading it to me. It had to be published. It should have been published all those years ago. The story should be out there. It was full of love, hope, and inspiration. My little door that my grandma had been talking about was when someone hits a blank wall in life. Mine had been there all along, looking at me straight in the face; I hadn't even noticed it!

> *When life becomes hard,*
> *And you hit a blank wall,*
> *Look closely,*
> *And you will find a little door.*

My little door looked me straight in the face for eighteen years. I had never acknowledged it, but even if I had, I'd have been too nervous to open it out of fear of what it may hold.

That Summer needed to be published, but how?

Chapter 4

I had a friend on Facebook who, a few years back, had mentioned to me he had a small publishing business. I contacted him through messenger and told him about my mum's book; he seemed pretty interested, and although there were many published books on child evacuees, *That Summer* was local and had a fascinating story slightly different from other books he had read. Could I send the manuscript in a Word document via email? I was lost at *Word*... what?

I was straight on the phone to Adam, who knew precisely what Tim meant. I handed Mum's manuscript to Adam, who scanned it onto the computer and started to format it. Still having Mum's box, which housed some photographs, Adam had carefully placed them into the autobiography with wording underneath. In hindsight, I'm so glad Adam had these photos, as they would have been damaged in the flood.

Adam sent me the manuscript so I could read through it and add comments. We had decided not to change it too much as it wouldn't be Mum's book. She wrote it as if she was talking. Working together on the manuscript and watching it come to life and turn into a book was terrific.

At last, it was ready to send to the publisher – Tim's company, *Viking Bay*. Tim phoned and thought it was great and set about getting it ready for publication. The book needed a cover. Adam had come up with the wording for the back, and we used Mum's summer painting of the poppy field painted of Hungerford Common in the fifties, and Adam used a photo of Mum with her sisters and two friends down Green Lane, where they had learned to swim, with a pill box behind them, indicating the war.

Tim suggested that I write an introduction explaining the story of the book, why I hadn't read it in the twenty odd years since she wrote it.

Here is the introduction to *That Summer*.

As a child, my mum would tell me stories about her childhood, and whenever we drove past the cottage, Mum would point out where she, my aunts, and grandparents lived as evacuees.

In her later life, Mum decided to turn the words into this book. Unfortunately, through grief and sadness of losing such a wonderful mother and friend, it has taken me 17 years to pick up the book and read it, and I have found it truly inspiring.

With the help and support of my son Adam, we have decided to publish the book in remembrance of my mum. "When you go through the hardest times and hit a blank wall, just look closely, and you will find a little door."

Sarah Roberts (née Warne)

Tim helped design posters, which I put up in and around Kintbury and Hungerford. He also printed Mum's four-season paintings and made them into four postcards, which could be used as bookmarks. The book *That Summer* was soon available to buy in paperback and hardback formats.

I cried when I received my copy of *That Summer*, and my heart went out to my Mum. My cousins and I all had a copy. The generation of my Mum and all her siblings passed away over the last eighteen years. The book held to our hearts and memories. It was all exciting and sad at the same time.

Tim had lots of contacts. Emails were coming through fast. An extract from *That Summer* was advertised on The virtual Hungerford Museum about how my family had been evacuated from Portsmouth to Hungerford and had stayed at The Church House. Mum had never mentioned it to me but had written about her days spent there in her book.

I didn't even know where The Church House was in Hungerford, so I drove to Hungerford to look for the building. Parking up to St. Lawrence's Church, I looked around and couldn't find the Church House. In front of the village green was a gloomy, old-looking building written on the plaque outside. It read Croft Hall, once Church House.

I saw people coming out of the building and mentioned to them that my mum had written a book about her memoirs. She and her family had been evacuated and had stayed in this building for six months. The congregation of people were highly interested and invited me in. It took my breath away. The old piano that Mavis had played on and sung as a child was still on the stage in the corner. I could imagine Betty tap dancing on the wooden stage and Gran sweating over the hot pans in the kitchen. Many people were asking questions about my family's evacuation. I answered what I knew; some bought the book as I'd brought quite a few and carried them around with me. I left the Croft Hall in shock at how awful it must have been for Mum and the family. No wonder Gran had wanted them to be able to return to Portsmouth as soon as possible. I think I would have struggled living there for six weeks! let alone six months!

On my way home towards Newbury, I posted a letter I had handwritten through the letterbox at Inglewood Cottage. Walking up the pathway after reading *That Summer* and the tales that had taken place here eighty years ago felt slightly strange. I had written in the letter that my mum had written a book and a lot of the story had taken place in and around the cottage. I was offering a book to the family living there, leaving my name and phone number, and was hoping for a reply. I had never entered Inglewood Cottage, but I knew it and had heard about Mum's adventures almost every week when we passed the road to Hungerford Common for a picnic with my cousins and Aunts when I was a child. No sooner had I returned home and put the kettle on when the phone rang. An elderly-sounding gentleman asked if I was Sarah and he had just opened my letter.

After seeing it advertised on one of the posters in the Kintbury post office and corner shop, the gentleman in question had already ordered and received the book. He invited me and my Cousins around for morning coffee. I said I would sign his copy of *That Summer* and bake an apple cake inspired by my Grans recipe from a wartime rationing recipe made from the Blenheim Apple tree mentioned in the book. Dr. Adams had said that would be lovely, although the old apple tree wasn't there anymore.

My cousins Cynthia, Jane, Julie, Alison, and I met at Kintbury and made our way towards the cottage, nervous but excited about how we would react or feel on our visit. I was wondering if the well was still there? Unfortunately, Sally and Christopher were at work and couldn't join us, and David was in Canada.
Making our way up the path towards the front door had a happy, warm sense around it.

Dr Robyn Adams welcomed us in. I imagined Mum entering the cottage as a small child, holding her one doll. She had been right. It did feel magical. We were welcomed into The Cottage and shown around. Nothing had changed. The large fireplace Mum had written about in *That Summer* was the same. Outside, propped up against the wall, was an old bathtub that was not in use but had the same description Mum had used. Could this have been the bathtub that our mums had sat in front of the fire during their stay here? Mum had also mentioned to me that they had used water from a corrugated metal water butt for a final hair rinse; the purities from the rainwater gave shine to the hair, which was still in use outside by the kitchen door. Cynthia surprised me when she showed us the room where she had been born. I had no idea she had been born in the cottage!

We enjoyed our chat and reminisced about our family history when Dr Adams asked us if we wanted to see the well. We followed him into a small room, the pantry. I had already been there to use the downstairs toilet and never noticed it. Robyn had explained that an indoor well was in the house deeds, but no one knew exactly where it was. When his wife was alive, they wanted to build a kitchen but needed to know where the indoor well was to continue their project. He told us that It wasn't until a year later that he met my mum by pure chance, who had shown them where the indoor well was.

My parents were walking past the cottage; they saw him with his late wife in the garden. Joyce had looked over the wall, introduced herself, and mentioned she and her family had been evacuated and lived in the cottage for eleven years. She had shown them where the well was. Yes, it was him that Mum had written about in the book *That Summer*. We were all amazed. This lovely gentleman had lived here at Inglewood Cottage since 1971.

But where was The Well?

"Here," said Robyn.

The floor felt slightly uneven, possibly covering a drain. We were shocked at how small the old indoor well was. It was only wide enough for two of us to stand over it at a time. There was no wall or barrier around, just a hole in the floor with a drain cover, and the bucket would have been tiny. No wonder our poor Grandma was constantly drawing water here. We were horrified to think she had used this well for ten years throughout the day. Eventually, ten years later, a tap was put in, but only when, on one occasion, Gran drew water up from the well and in the bucket contained a dead rat.

She looked after her sickly husband and five young children with her one dress, washing it at night and putting it on in the morning once it had dried, leaving her beautiful house in Portsmouth with her mod cons to this. Gran had never once moaned about her hardship, and after seeing the well, I was thankful for everything.

Chapter 5

I was invited for an interview with Penny Locke on a local radio station, 4 Legs Radio – so called because it's based in Lambourn, known as the valley of the racehorse. I was a little nervous, but she was a great interviewer, and I soon relaxed and got into the flow of talking. My original twenty-minute allocated time ran on to forty.

Tim invited me to a Farmers Market he had organised, held in an open courtyard with various sellers. Meeting many people interested in Mum's book was an excellent opportunity. Julie and Alison, my cousins, came to support me. While sitting at the trestle table, Julie and I noticed a white feather that landed gently at our feet; it was a comforting niceness. Our gran had always said a single white feather is a sign from a loved one who has passed over.

After this book signing, I was asked if I would like to chat with a local journalist, Paul Allen, on his podcast. The show was on for over an hour, and I was a little bit anxious as there were a lot of listeners.

I gave a talk at Audley, Inglewood, a retirement home half a mile from Inglewood Cottage, with Cynthia at my side. When Mum and her family had lived at the cottage, Audley was a monastery, then Inglewood Health Hydro, until it was modernised to a higher-end retirement home, utilising and leaving the natural spa and health hydro to be used by the residents and members who were over fifty-five years old.

Penny Locke had phoned me to ask if I would like to go back on her radio show, but this time to talk about the food rationing during the war, mentioned in the book. She asked if I would make my gran's World War Two apple cake and bread and butter pudding and to also talk about how Gran had made butter. The show would also feature two chefs. We would be discussing the diets of yesteryear compared to modern-day Britain. I only had fifteen minutes of airtime to promote Mum's book but I was looking forward to the show.

When I arrived at the studio with the apple cakes and bread pudding using Gran's recipes, Penny had informed me that one of the chefs couldn't make it, so it would be one other guest and me, but just before we went on air, nobody else had turned up. It would just be Penny and I. She started by introducing the show and then played an extra song. I sat on her side of the desk. We ad-libbed and talked about how much healthier diets were during the war and how much blander food had tasted compared to today's food, which contained fewer flavourings and additives; no wonder people were on a healthier diet during the war years.

The show came over very well, and afterward, Penny invited me to The Hungerford Artisan Market, which would be held at the field next to Hungerford Croft Hall the following week.

It was a beautiful day, and the artisan fayre was next door to The Croft Hall; my stall was the first one you would come to with the *That Summer* books on display and Gran's recipes. I would hand out bread and butter pudding and apple cake samples. I dressed in clothes from World War Two and picked up a £1:50 apron covered in red apples from a charity shop. Adam came along for the support. While there, I met Tamara, who ran stalls in the area and invited me to hold a stall at The Jubilee Hall; my cousin Jane came to support me.

Mum had worked at Ginchey Hair, and her former colleagues all wanted a copy of her autobiography, too, and they could remember Mum writing down her memories and ideas on memo sticks while sitting at the reception desk. I couldn't believe how far this inspirational book was taking me.

I was in the Newbury Weekly News, and on the website Newbury Today, I was invited onto Kennet Radio. I was asked to talk at Women's Institutes at The Royal British Legions. Hungerford Book Shop started to stock *That Summer*. I was a guest on BBC Radio Berkshire twice in one month on different shows. I loved the limelight just to think I had never wanted to open that blue folder, let alone read Mum's manuscript. All the interviewers had thought the book would make a great film or documentary that would have been amazing, but I would need to figure out where to start with that idea.

One of my interviews was very close to my heart. A lady had contacted me from a charity called *My Speaker Friend*, who asked to meet me and allow *That Summer* to be turned into an audio book for people in care homes. I remember my gran listening to audiobooks. I was delighted to help.

Sue came to my cottage with her machine and introduced me to the Dictaphone. Sue would narrate the book, and I would introduce it. I hoped the audience would find *That Summer* delightful to listen to as much as I did to read. I imagined my gran sitting in her armchair next to her Rayburn, listening intently.

Me and my cousins, with *That Summer*

Inglewood Cottage

Dr Robyn Adams with me and my cousins

Hungerford Bookshop

I am really looking forward to prerecording another Paul Presents Podcast with Sarah E Roberts to chat about a book she has had published. The book is called "That Summer" A true story of wartime evacuation to Kintbury from the memories Of Sarah's mum

Christine Live & Local
Sunday 18 Sept 10-12pm
Text 07418 310 210
www.kennetradio.com

Interview with Mark Summers raising awareness & funds for

THREE PEAKS WALK
SEPTEMBER 2022
www.justgiving.com/fundraising/marksummers-alkingtoraiseforms

Sarah Roberts talks to Christine about an amazing new book.
That Summer.
A true story of wartime to Kintbury Jussie E Lilliot

 Puppy tips with Anthony Hewitt
www.juniperdogs.com

 What's on with Paul Allen
www.westberksvillagers.com

Playing a selection of great music

Kennet Radio

Signing with Adam at Croft Hall

With Penny at Four Legs Radio

The year was coming to a close. I was book signing at the Christmas fayre in St. Mary's Church, Kintbury, when a couple of people started to ask me about what happened next to my family after *That Summer*, which surprised me. The book didn't need anything else or a follow-up, and Mum wasn't around anymore to write it. Adam and some friends had suggested I should write a follow-up book...

Chapter 6

It was January, and I was back in St. Mary's Church with a New Year Stall. I always found peace and strength in the church of St. Mary's at Kintbury, where my christening took place on September 26th, 1965. Who would have thought thirty-nine years later, on the same date, that my mum would have passed away?

I soon realised I might have exhausted the market for *That Summer*. So many people had bought a copy and been fascinated by mum's story, and wanted to know what happened next! While sipping my latte, I decided my book would be called *Lost Summers of Days Gone By*.

I felt excited by the thought. I would use Mum's painting *Autumn Weir* as the book cover and write the follow-up story of Mum's life until my gran passed away. A buyer approached me saying they had loved reading *That Summer* and asked if there would be another book. I heard myself blurt out, "Oh yes, the book should be out before the summer; it will be called *Lost Summers of Days Gone By*."

"Fantastic," was the reply, and they wanted to put an order in there and then!

I had never written a book before, only at school, but that was long ago. I was fifty-seven years old, but it would be good for me to do. Tim was very supportive, and so was Adam, along with my cousins and friends.

Adam had given me my dad's side of my family tree and an old map of the area around The Newbury Corn Exchange, where Dad had been born in one of the five corn cottages behind the large building.

I remembered my childhood and interviewed my cousins about our past and growing up. I researched information to ensure the history I had written was correct for my book to come together. I also interviewed Dorothy, who was now back living in Newbury after thirty-two years in Florida. She had worked at Dreweatt, Barton and Watson's, who held the auction for the cattle market in old Newbury Town, which now known as The Urban Village

had been built on the site. I interviewed Dorothy's sister, Ros, who is 95 years old and was born and bred in Newbury.
Cousin Sally had one of Mum's paintings of the bluebell woods, which Mum had painted in West Woods Marlborough. I asked Tim if he could create bookmarks using the painting.

I did nothing else with my time, and the book was soon written. After many hours of preparation, *Lost Summers* was available in paperback and a luxury colour hardback edition.

I was very proud. I had used my maiden name, Warne. I hoped it would have made my parents proud too. I was back again on Four Legs Radio with Penny Locke. I visited Radio Kennet at their studios at Clock Tower House in Newbury, for a live broadcast. They asked if there would be a third book – I said no – famous last words!

I was doing more signings than ever. People were wanting more. We were a small, simple family that had been caught up in The Blitz and fought for survival. Hungerford Book Shop had wanted to sell *Lost Summers* alongside *That Summer* as it had also accumulated a lot of interest. People loved the true stories of life in an ordinary but colourful family.

That morning, I was doing a talk in Kintbury, and Shirley, a friend from the village, had assisted me with my book signing.

Many people were there and were asking lots of questions. One question that kept arising was, will you write another book? I replied with a definite *No!*

A man approached me as Shirley and I were packing up. He told me he had written a book and had self-published it on Amazon. It made me think: I had enjoyed writing my book, and people loved reading it and still wanted more. On the way back to the car, I mentioned it to Shirley but added I wouldn't know what to write about. She had replied that an idea would come up when I was least thinking about it. She was right. On visiting Adam, I mentioned that people were still interested in *That Summer* and *Lost Summers of Days Gone By*.

Part 3
Summers End

Chapter 1

Over a coffee, I asked Adam what he thought about me writing another book and if he could develop any inspirational ideas. He replied with his dimpled smile, beautiful straight teeth, and brown eyes; although six feet tall, he reminded me of my mum in many ways.

"I've got just the thing," he went upstairs and, within a few minutes, was carrying a huge box, the one Dad had offered to me when Mum had passed away. It had been the contents of her college writings and artwork.

"Here," he said, putting the box on the floor." I thought one day you might like this." I opened it, and to my surprise, the contents contained The Lilliott family tree that my Aunty Doris had researched from Somerset House those thirty-eight years ago!

There were photos of my grandma, her family, Sheerwater Farm, The Grove Ferry, and the list went on. Some of these articles were the ones that had been in the original crate from my Grandma's house when we had gathered around Aunty Joan's wooden kitchen table when Mum had started to look into our Lilliott family past starting at Ash, Kent, and then Australia.

There was even an article Mum had written about her visit to Portsmouth on a coach trip with Aunty Mavis. The family road they had lived on before their evacuation had changed its name from Shore Avenue to Moorings Way, and my grandad's local public house, The Good Companion, was still standing. This I must visit.

I took the box home with a new insight. This box contained so much historical content, some dating back to the seventh century, with some lettering fading. I knew something positive was necessary.

I contacted Newbury College and put myself on a computer course, along with English grammar and punctuation. I had also met a lady at one of my talks, and she had asked me if I would visit her and others at a creative writing group she attended on a Friday morning called West Berkshire Writers with *That Summer* and *Lost Summers*. She thought both books were captivating and wanted to read more. After meeting the group and sharing my family's inspiration and hopeful dreams, I was asked if I'd like to join them. I was delighted. I would start writing *Summer Rainbows* at my own pace. There was a lot of research to do, but there was only me this time.

With Mum's memoirs from the box, I placed them all in date order with Mum's biographies from the box. At the very bottom of the pile was a rose-printed covered book in A4 size that I'd never seen before, and on opening it, I realised it wasn't finished; the book was half empty.

It was written in Mum's neatest handwriting, full of proverbs, some well-known and some of her own, and beautifully decorated. A book filled with hope and joy, or as I call it, *A Book of Hope and Joyce*.

When we have done all the work we were sent to earth to do; we are allowed to shed our body which imprisons our soul like a cocoon encloses the future butterfly. And when the time is right, we can let go of it and we will be free of pain, free of fears and worries — free as a beautiful butterfly, returning home to God.

Hope effects everything, let your hook always be cast. In the stream where you least expect it, there will be a fish. (Ovid)

An expert at anything was once a beginner.

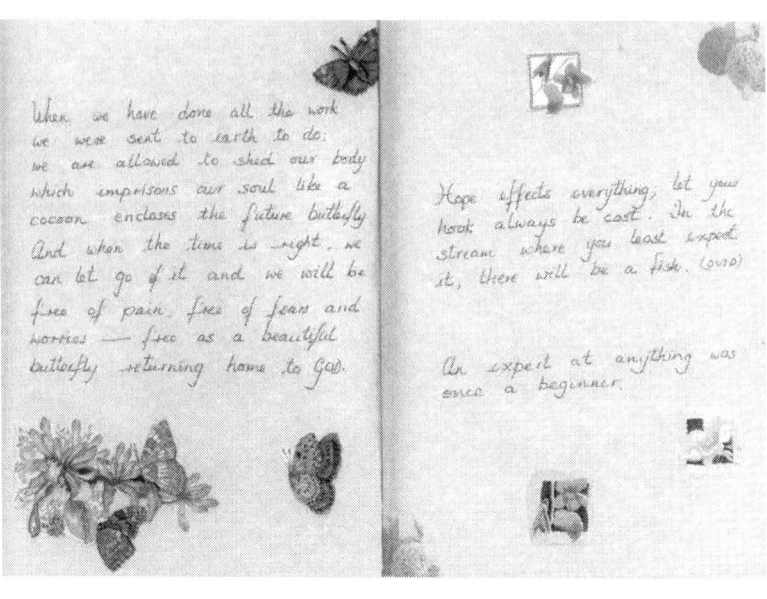

IN FLANDERS FIELDS

THE POPPIES GROW

We only get out of our tea bowl what we put into it.
(an old Chinese proverb)

It is always the unexpected that comes to pass.

To joy intensely one must have suffered first.

The future belongs to those who believe in the beauty of their dreams.

Sometimes what seems to be a big tragedy turns out to become the greatest good in our lives, you value life in a new way.

Do not fight against the whirlpool when cast into it, but move with it to survive.
(Chinese proverb).

IT is best to bend with the wind when it blows.

Take what you want from life and pay the price.
(Spanish proverb)

Sometimes nothing seems worthwhile but then from out of the blue, something happens to lighten your life like being shown a different path.

A bee can move an Ox.

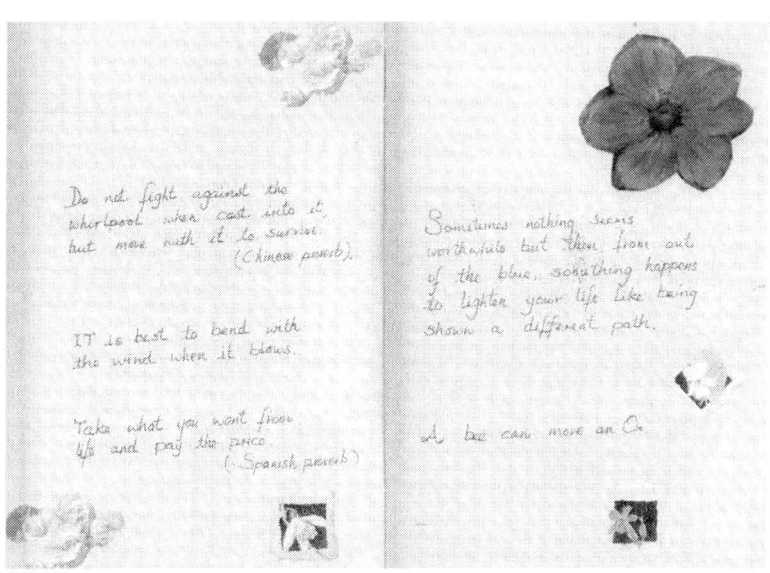

Happiness is like a butterfly, chase after it and you will never catch it but if you sit quietly in the shade it will come to sit on your shoulder.

Weeping may endure for a night but joy cometh in the morning. (Solomon)

In his heart, a man plans his course, but the Lord determines his steps.
(Proverbs 16:9)

Faith is the fabric of life.

Live each day as you would climb a mountain. Keep the goal in mind but enjoy the scenery.

One picture is worth a hundred thousand words.
(Chinese proverb)

Chapter 2

I Googled the pub The Good Companion, and to my surprise, it was still there! The landlord, Scott, had told me on the phone where the public house was between Eastern Avenue and at the end of Moorings Way, once Shore Avenue. I then knew I had the right place.

On arrival on Moorings Way, I was in shock as there was no sea but a road with houses on each side, a housing estate, and a block of flats called Shearwater; what a coincidence, as my gran was born in Sheerwater Farm. I walked along Moorings Way. It looked unrecognisable from the way Mum had described the area. I arrived at no.23. A driveway and a garage replaced the archway. The house was for sale. I walked up the concrete path with the gate on one hinge, hanging open. I went into the garden. The Anderson shelter had now gone, of course, but there was a slight raise on the grass; perhaps it was under there. I had no one to ask and wish I'd never visited. I wanted to keep my mum's memories in my heart, but now that I was here, my memories would differ significantly.

A friendly neighbour came out and asked if he could help. I explained to him that my mum and her family had once lived in this house eighty years ago and had evacuated during The Blitz. My Grandma thought they would only be away for a few weeks, and alas, they couldn't return as WW2 raged on a lot longer than she had thought. I explained to the neighbour that Mum had said Shore Avenue had been on the seafront. It had confused me to see this housing estate, and I thought maybe I would see the remnants of the Anderson shelter she had mentioned in her childhood tales.

He had replied that the Anderson shelters had been removed straight after the war, popping back into his house and asking me to stay there. He soon returned holding a book with photos showing me the now and how the area had once looked when Mum had lived there.

At the end of the road was Milton Common, and reclaimed land was formed between 1962 and 1970 when a chalk and clay bund was built across the mouth of the lake, and the combined area was progressively drained and filled with domestic refuse and other waste including building rubble to old cars and water tanks. It was a huge reclamation exercise. The city's Second World War rubble was also used to fill this massive area. This was later capped and grassed over to form Milton Common. It is an area of 46 hectares south of Great Salterns Quay, bounded by Eastern Road, Moorings Way, and Langstone Harbour. The reformed land was formed by filling in a large lake called Milton Lake and is now a conservation area. No wonder Mum and Mavis hadn't spoken much about their visit here.

The Good Companion was only ten houses away from the family home.

I didn't realise how close it was. Scott, the landlord, was accommodating and told me about the pub's history, pointing out the extensions added onto the pub and its original building and showing me the part of the car park that was once underwater. I could imagine my gran and grandad (a man I had never met) in the pub garden with Mum and her siblings sipping lemonade and my gran with her Guinness.

from the original photos I had seen of the school, and I posted a copy of *That Summer* through the letterbox along with Mum's postcards and a cover letter. Ongoing with my thoughts and stepping into my mum's lost childhood, I made my way to

Commercial Road to find the tragic place, the Woolworths, where my grandma had been shopping until her purse was mislaid in the jostling crowds. She had been so close to losing her life in 1941 when the building had been destroyed by military aircraft. I sat to drink a coffee, absorbing my thoughts and trying to imagine how fearful life was once here, but I had nothing in my life to compare with that fear. I asked a lady walking by if she knew where Woolworths had been. She answered me straight away and pointed at the new build, now Primark.

The dockyard was next, my approach taking the no.23 bus. I was soon there. It amazed me that the road from the dockyard where my grandad had worked was Queens Road, where they had stayed when they were first married, moving from Kent to here, and where Joan had lived before moving to Ebdon Road after losing Doris and Ronnie.

Walking towards the large dockyard and its wondrous old buildings of naval and historic history, I entered one of the buildings, asking about its past and telling of how my granddad had worked here and how the family evacuated during the blitz. The staff there were highly interested in my news and asked if I would mind being interviewed and having it recorded in their history records. I emerged an hour later.

It had been a long day, and I'd booked in for an evening meal at The Good Companion, but I still had time to visit Kingston Cemetery. There was no way I could visit Portsmouth without visiting the graves of Doris and Ronnie. I had phoned Milton cemetery offices to find the exact location of their burial. I was glad I had, as in the eighties, the cemetery department had removed the pavings from children's graves buried over a hundred years ago, as the grass in that part of the cemetery needed to be kept short and neat as a memorial was built in that area of the cemetery to remember the servicemen and women who had fought and lost their lives in the war. The lady I had spoken to on the phone had emailed me a map locating their plot.

When I eventually found the grave by a sheltered wall, overcome with emotion as when my grandparents decided to billet their family for safety as a temporary measure, little did they know that they would never return and be able to tend their children's graves ever again. How heart-wrenching it must have been to leave when they had once visited their lost loved ones every day. I pulled out from my carrier bag a small sodden piece of dirt that I had removed from my grandparents' grave in Kintbury and replaced and replanted the earth onto their children's graves.

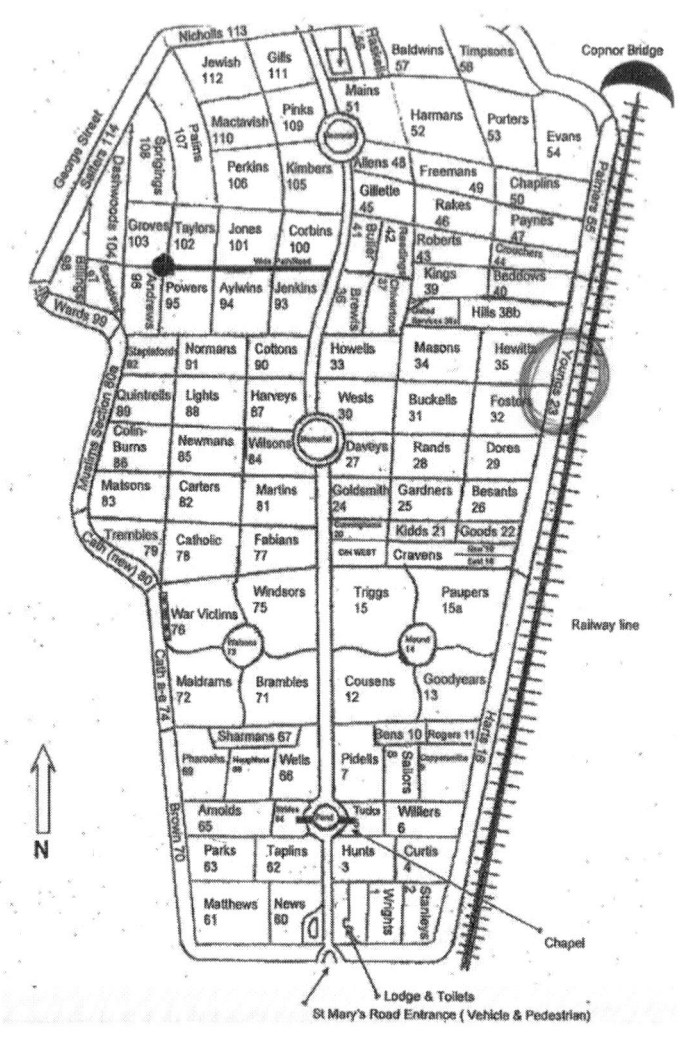

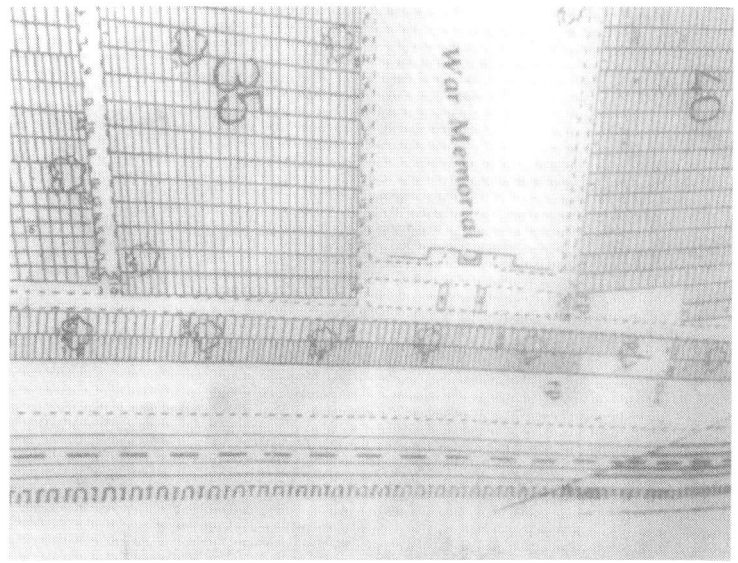

Making my way back to The Good Companion was a good feeling.

The following morning, the sky saw dark clouds, bringing torrential rain with them. I was glad I visited the places I had wanted to visit yesterday. Before leaving the area, I wanted to visit St. Mary's church, where Mum and her siblings had been christened. The Sunday service had just finished. I had no idea how stunning this building was: the vastness and wonder of the inside and the welcoming congregation. It took me aback, and *That Summer* posters were placed in the church's welcoming area after coffee and chat. I was invited back to hold a stall at The Church Christmas Fayre the following month.

The last stop was to drop off some books to Jo, who wanted to stock *That Summer* in her local bookshop called "New to You" on Cosham Road.

On Route, I passed where The Cosham Cottage Homes on Southwick Road had once stood, where Mum and her siblings, all but Joan, had stayed while their parents were recovering from Ill health in separate hospitals.

The homes were closed in 1968, and most of the buildings were demolished. The former administrative block was converted for residential living until 2015.

During the four years of the Portsmouth Blitz, Portsmouth officially suffered 67 air raids in which 930 people were killed, 1,216 people were hospitalised, and a further 1,621 people were injured. Approximately 6,000 homes were damaged, and nearly 69,000 houses received some form of minor bomb damage. It is also estimated that 6,300 residences were destroyed.

The night Mum had been inspired to write her poem 'Stars' was January 10/11/1941, Which had also been the night Gran had decided for the whole family to evacuate Portsmouth. According to German records, as many as 40,000 incendiary devices were dropped during that major overnight raid. It was one of the heaviest attacks, and approximately 300 German aircraft attacked Portsmouth, dropping 350 tons of high explosives.

In one night, there were 171 deaths, 430 people injured, and 3,000 people were made homeless. The first stick of bombs hit the electricity station, which plunged the city into darkness; there was no electricity for four days afterward. Fires burned for twelve hours as the water mains had also been hit, making firefighting impossible. Significant damage was caused on Commercial Road, Palmerston Road, and Kings Road. Old Portsmouth and Portsmouth Guildhall were virtually destroyed by fire when incendiaries hit them. The first effects of the raid were seen from a point seven miles away, which had looked like a curtain of flares and, over time, merged into one large patch of a deep red light that occasionally flickered into a bowl of smoke and cloud.

Also that night, buildings, including schools, churches, hotels, business premises, and a hospital, were damaged or destroyed.

Chapter 3

The next few weeks after visiting Portsmouth were a whirlwind. Meon school had thanked me for posting *That Summer* and Mum's paintings. The school held an assembly for the evacuated children from Portsmouth who never returned.

Tim had phoned to say he had made *That Summer* available on Amazon. It was fantastic news and would open many more doors for me. Within one week of *That Summer* being on Amazon, the book had received five-star ratings. Both books were also placed in the Oxford Bodleian Library. What would my mum have thought?

After visiting Portsmouth, my next place to visit would be my grandma's place of birth, Sheerwater Farm, Ash, Kent. The Grove Ferry Public House was now a bed and breakfast. I booked a room, excited, not knowing what to expect.

The day drew near. I was thankful for Google Maps. I don't know how Mum managed to find where and who when she had visited the area over twenty years prior. Places were so much easier to find in today's world.

After driving the 167-mile journey, I felt the time had stopped, and I had travelled back into the nineteenth century. There were no high rise buildings or even modern-day superstores.

In the open fields with nowhere fenced off, there grew leafy green cabbages and cauliflower, with orchards of red, rosy apples and strawberries growing in abundance. I never realised places like this were still in existence. Mum couldn't understand why her Mother had left this idyllic Kent Countryside, and now I was also left wondering why.

The Grove Ferry pub came into view as I drove over the railway track. I could imagine Gran standing at the station as a child. Next to the station was a bridge originally built in 1932 to replace the chain ferry over The River Stour. Looking closely at both sides of the riverbank, one can still see the sloping banks where Mr. Bing, the Ferry Man, managed the chain ferry to transport passengers from one side of the river to the other. He would charge a half penny for foot passengers, tuppence for four-wheeled carts, thruppence for other wagons, and additional charges for sheep, cattle, etc.

The ferry was a pontoon affair, with hinged flaps at both ends, which ran up the sloping banks as the ferry pulled in. The River Stour was tidal there and varied in width. Motive power was just by the ferryman. There was a steel cable across the river, which had passed between well-oiled pulley wheels on the white posts at either end of the flat deck and the ferryman stood with his back to it, pulling on it with his arms and pushing with his legs onto the ferry deck. Most times, the passengers would lend a hand.

In the adjacent fields, lavender shrubs had grown commercially over several acres beside the road when approaching the river from Preston.

John, the landlord, greeted me and showed extreme interest in the book I was writing and about my family history. To my amazement, there were still Lilliotts farming in the area.

Once refreshed and settled in, I journeyed around the hamlets. I had visions of my Great-Grandfather, Thomas Southee Lilliott, tramping from one hamlet to another, carrying his giant bible under his arm. I passed Chislet Church, where my grandparents were married. Into Preston, I stopped by a corner shop and chatted with a few locals. What friendly people. I felt I had known them all my life. Driving on, I saw the cottage where Nan Barlow had lived. The postcard Nan sent to my mum looked the same today as it was then. Gran's school was still a school.

Making my way towards Sheerwater Farm, I could imagine the first time my Mum visited with Betty, Julie, and June. I stopped at the cottage and had an overwhelming urge to cry. How I missed my Grandma, how she would cover my face with butterfly kisses and her Tinkerbell laugh, and how she would call me her little lamb and listen to me read. I wonder what she would have thought of my last book and the present one I was working on.

I had a strong urge to knock on the door. A couple came outside and welcomed me in, explaining they had received a phone call from the local shop telling them I might be stopping there. Kate invited me in and showed me around the cottage. The inglenook fireplace was still there. Alas, the dairy where Gran and her mother, Sarah Ann Castle, had once patted butter into shape was now a bathroom, and the original flag-tiled flooring had been replaced with a modernised version.

Kate had a large box containing documentation about Sheerwater Farm through the ages and even had parchment strips of hand-painted wallpaper that had once covered the farmhouse walls. Kate and her husband showed me photos of the plans and deeds of the cottage and loved that there was a book with photographs covering some of the area's past. Kate put *That Summer* in the Sheerwater Farm box among the history with the rest of the collection. Mum's book would always stay here with Sheerwater Farm. The garden was still the same as Gran had described with its apple orchard. I thanked the couple as I journeyed to Hop Farm and Westerham to the marshes, promising Kate I would keep in touch and return next year.

Sheerwater Farm 2023

Driving back towards the pub, I passed St. Nicholas Church, Ash, where Thomas Southee and Sarah Ann Castle were buried. St. Nicholas at Ash was probably built around 1190 AD on the site of an early Saxon building, which was altered in the 14th century, and its central tower added in the 15th century. The prominent tower and steeple, which now house a ring of ten bells, were once used as navigation aids. Inside the church is a collection of medieval monumental effigies, and amongst the brasses, one from 1455 AD reveals a unique horseshoe headdress.

On return to The Grove Ferry, a couple called Chris and Shirley were waiting for me. It had been mentioned to them both that a Lilliott relation was visiting the area to research her grandmother's family tree and was looking to find Hook Farm at Grove Corner, or Grove Farm, as my gran had said. It was the farm where my great-granddad Thomas Southee had worked after falling ill and giving up Sheerwater Farm. His brother, Joseph Lilliott, had owned Grove Farm, or Hook Farm, as it was now named. Chris and Shirley had bought the farm from Gilbert Lilliott, or Bert, as he was better known. When Bert sold the farm, he kept the land. Chris and Shirley invited me back to their home at Hook Farm.

The farmhouse was much larger than I had expected and significantly modernised. However, there was an original red tiled flooring in a room that looked like it could have been a dairy or even where the Lilliotts may have kept their produce. It struck me that there was also an indoor well in this room. I had only come across the one before that, which was at Inglewood Cottage.

Upstairs, looking out, I was told all the surrounding fields I could see were still owned and farmed by the Lilliotts. As I was shown around, I thought of my Gran with her siblings and Helen Griggs with her daughter Nan Barlow. How wonderful and peaceful a time it must have been to have experienced this livelihood.

Outside, the original barn still stood where, over one hundred and twenty-five years ago, Gran and her sisters had sat with the trestle tables laden with strawberries and cream. Thanking the couple, I made my way back towards The Grove Ferry.

I parked, and as I made my way into the bar, I noticed a woman standing there with the most piercing blue eyes and her fair hair thick with waves. A Lilliot trait, my gran had always said.

"Out of all of my seven children, Ronnie was the only one to be born with the Lilliott looks of piercing blue eyes and thick blonde wavy hair."

The woman introduced herself as Catherine, Joseph Lilliotts's great-granddaughter. I was overjoyed. It was so lovely to meet and chat with her. Catherine told me that her grandad, Bert Lilliott, had three daughters; her mother, Brenda, was the eldest, then Monica and Norma. When her granddad had the farm, she knew of the wonderful family Christmases held there; she knew of the Barlows, the Griggs, and the Faggs. Before Gilbert had passed away, although he had sold Hook Farm, he had kept the land, passing it on evenly to his three daughters, and now their children, including Catherine, had inherited a piece of land each. Catherine told me the family was still growing and harvesting strawberries and potatoes, which the Lilliotts transported to local fish and chips shops.

Nothing has changed here since Gran was born. I gave Catherine a copy of *That Summer*. Now, the Lilliott family will always have a copy. We will keep in touch, that's for sure.

Where Mr. Bing, The Ferryman, once pulled the chain ferry.

Later that afternoon, I quietly sat alone at the Riverside of The Stour, reminiscing. With the trilogy of books - *That Summer*, *Lost*

Summers of Days Gone By, and *Summer Rainbows* - the story had now come full circle. It had begun here when a young man came looking for his fortune, my great great grandfather, Edward Lilliott, son of Thomas Lilliott, born in 1778 of a family believed to be of Huguenot stock, who had carried all his possessions in a red handkerchief on a stick.

Gran had always said. "Life often looks like a blank wall, but when you come right up to it, you will see a little door."

My little door had been staring me in the face for twenty years. I had been frightened of opening it, but when I did, the door opened, giving me a new lease of life and leading me to opportunities, discoveries and adventures. I hope this book will inspire you to open your little door, as you never know where it will take you.

Epilogue

One morning, early in 2024, as I was watching GMTV and Gyles Brandreth, who was a guest on the show, was talking about his friend Queen Camilla's love of reading. He said that Her Majesty would soon be launching a podcast called "The Queens Reading Room". On a whim, I decided to phone Buckingham Palace to ask if The Queen would be interested to read That Summer. I was transferred to Her Majesty's secretary, so I explained how it had come about; that it had taken me twenty years to read after my mum passing away and how I had now the book published. I also mentioned the following two books, *Lost Summers* and *Summer Rainbows*.

To my surprise, the lady on the phone appeared extremely interested and asked for me to write everything I had mentioned into a letter for Her Majesty, also adding that she was sure she would be very interested. I immediately put pen to paper and posted my letter.

I wasn't expecting a reply so soon, but just under two weeks an envelope addressed to me, and clearly from Buckingham Palace. On the back of the envelope was the red stamp of The Royal Crest. I was excited … I was ecstatic! The letter, printed on beautiful paper, was headed with the Royal Crest, and written underneath in bold red ink was BUCKINGHAM PALACE. It was from The Deputy Private Secretary to Her Majesty The Queen. I will treasure it.

The letter was thanking me on behalf Queen Camilla. It said that she was very interested in reading about my mum and her family during the war and asked if I might like to send a copy for her, adding that "this comes with The Queen's warmest thanks and best wishes".

I could imagine my mum reading the letter out to my gran, as they sat in front of Gran's Rayburn. Gran would have cleared her throat and would have said.
  "Well I never, Jussie!"

An Extract from the Lilliott Family Tree

No. 2. Lilliott Family Groups from 1811 to 1909.

1. Thomas Lilliott married married Elizabeth S. White Ap. 18th 1811. She died in 1821 and he in 1832. Their children were – Elizabeth, born June 4th 1812 who died unmarried March 7th 1896; Susannah, born April 2nd 1814 who died a few months before her father; Thomas Souther, born Nov. 25th 1816, who died May 31st 1822; Edward Lilliott, born Nov. 11th 1818, who died Aug 15th 1886; And Ann born Jan 16th 1821 who died unmarried May 6th 1848.

II – Edward Lilliott married Sarah Perkins June 21st, 1842. She died Feb. 23rd 1864, and he married Jane Shilling May 9th, 1865. He died August 15th 1886. Their children were – Edward, born May 14th 1848; Joseph, born June 9th, 1850; Anne Elizabeth born Feb 25th 1853, who died Feb 17th 1895; Sarah Ann, born Feb 4th, 1855, who died April 24th 1908; Mary Ellen, born Aug 24th 1856, who died May 1st 1885; Thomas Souther, born Oct 21st 1860; John Perkins, born Nov 18th 1862, died Sep. 1873; Frank, born Feb 16, 1866; Rose, born Oct 27th, 1867, died Sep. 1873; Richard born June 18th, 1873; and William George, born Sep 8th 1874.

III – Joseph Lilliott married Helen Cox Culmer Dec 2nd 1873; She died Mar. 15th 1901 and he married Jane Elvery Oct 15th 1902. Their children: – Alfred Joseph, born Oct 10th 1874; Annie, born

The First Book

That Summer

A true story of wartime evacuation to Kintbury

Jussie E. Lilliot

'That Summer' is an inspirational, true account of a young girl's perspective on life as an evacuee during the Blitz. Those days, events and experiences would have a long-lasting effect and come to shape her whole life. Beautifully told, with stories, photographs and records of family roots dating back to the sixteenth century and a return to her childhood safe haven - the village of Kintbury, Berkshire - this window into British life during World War 2 portrays multi-generational hardships and tribulations that have spanned the centuries.

While her family's world would collapse and be reshaped, the one constant strength that stayed true throughout was the love, devotion and loyalty they had for each other. Jussie's story is one of enduring hope, where no matter how hard life can be, there is still joy and happiness to be found right around the corner.

Available from www.vikingbay.co.uk and Amazon

The Second Book

Lost Summers follows "That Summer" by Jussie E. Lilliot - the true story of an evacuated family from Portsmouth who found a safe haven in the village of Kintbury, Berkshire, during World War II. Written through the eyes of Jussie's daughter Sarah, the book explores the lives of the family after the war and how they moved on to make new lives, with marriages and their own children. The love within the family is ever-present, as post-war Britain changes through the decades, with life in Kintbury retaining its rural charm.

Lost Summers not only details a family life that will be familiar to anyone who grew up in those transformative decades, it's a fascinating first-person view of Newbury and Kintbury during the 1960s and 70s, and is richly illustrated with family photos and vivid stories.

Available from www.vikingbay.co.uk and Amazon

Printed in Great Britain
by Amazon

37722322R00097